THE IMPORTANCE OF

Napoleon Bonaparte

by
Bob Carroll

Lucent Books, P.O. Box 289011, San Diego, CA 92198-9011

These and other titles are included in The Importance Of biography series:

Cleopatra	Margaret Mead
Christopher Columbus	Michelangelo
Marie Curie	Wolfgang Amadeus Mozart
Thomas Edison	Napoleon Bonaparte
Albert Einstein	Richard M. Nixon
Benjamin Franklin	Jackie Robinson
Galileo Galilei	Anwar Sadat
Thomas Jefferson	Margaret Sanger
Chief Joseph	Mark Twain
Malcolm X	H.G. Wells

Library of Congress Cataloging-in-Publication Data

Carroll, Bob, 1936–
    Napoleon Bonaparte/ by Bob Carroll.
        p. cm.—(The Importance of)
    Includes bibliographical references and index.
    Summary: A biography of the general who used his skills to carve out the largest and wealthiest empire the world had seen since the fall of Rome.
    ISBN 1-56006-021-2 (alk. paper)
    1. Napoleon I, Emperor of the French, 1769–1821— Juvenile literature. 2. France—History—Consulate and Empire, 1799–1815—Juvenile literature. 3. France—Kings and rulers—Biography—Juvenile literature. [1. Napoleon I, Emperor of the French, 1769–1821. 2. Kings, queens, rulers, etc. 3. Generals.] I. Title. II. Series.
DC203.C223   1994
944.05—dc20   93-17852
[B]   CIP

Copyright 1994 by Lucent Books, Inc., P.O. Box 289011, San Diego, California, 92198-9011

Contents

Important Dates in the Life of
Napoleon Bonaparte   4
Foreword   5

INTRODUCTION
The Great Adventure   6

CHAPTER 1
An Emperor and a King   9

CHAPTER 2
For Patriotism   21

CHAPTER 3
Fortune's Favorite   33

CHAPTER 4
To Italy and Egypt   44

CHAPTER 5
The First Consul   56

CHAPTER 6
The Emperor Strikes   67

CHAPTER 7
Decline   77

CHAPTER 8
Fall   88

EPILOGUE
A Mixed Legacy   100

Notes   103
For Further Reading   105
Works Consulted   106
Index   108
Picture Credits   111
About the Author   112

Important Dates in the Life of Napoleon Bonaparte

Born at Ajaccio, Corsica. — **1769**

Saves Convention with "a whiff of grapeshot." — **1795**

1796 — Marries Josephine de Beauharnais.

Forces Austria to sign Treaty of Campo Formio. — **1797**

1799 — Seizes power in France as First Consul.

Crowns himself emperor of the French. — **1804**

1805 — Defeats allied armies of the Austrians and Russians at the Battle of Austerlitz.

Battle of Trafalgar. — **1806**

1807 — Defeats Prussians at Jena and Auerstadt.

Defeats Russians at Friedland. —

1810 — Marries Marie Louise of Austria.

Retreats from Moscow. — **1812**

Abdicates throne; exile to Elba. — **1814**

1815 — Returns to power; loses at Waterloo; exile to St. Helena.

Dies on St. Helena. — **1821**

Foreword

THE IMPORTANCE OF biography series deals with individuals who have made a unique contribution to history. The editors of the series have deliberately chosen to cast a wide net and include people from all fields of endeavor. Individuals from politics, music, art, literature, philosophy, science, sports, and religion are all represented. In addition, the editors did not restrict the series to individuals whose accomplishments have helped change the course of history. Of necessity, this criterion would have eliminated many whose contribution was great, though limited. Charles Darwin, for example, was responsible for radically altering the scientific view of the natural history of the world. His achievements continue to impact the study of science today. Others, such as Chief Joseph of the Nez Percé, played a pivotal role in the history of their own people. While Joseph's influence does not extend much beyond the Nez Percé, his nonviolent resistance to white expansion and his continuing role in protecting his tribe and his homeland remain an inspiration to all.

These biographies are more than factual chronicles. Each volume attempts to emphasize an individual's contributions both in his or her own time and for posterity. For example, the voyages of Christopher Columbus opened the way to European colonization of the New World. Unquestionably, his encounter with the New World brought monumental changes to both Europe and the Americas in his day. Today, however, the broader impact of Columbus's voyages is being critically scrutinized. *Christopher Columbus,* as well as every biography in The Importance Of series, includes and evaluates the most recent scholarship available on each subject.

Each author includes a wide variety of primary and secondary source quotations to document and substantiate his or her work. All quotes are footnoted to show readers exactly how and where biographers derive their information, as well as provide stepping stones to further research. These quotations enliven the text by giving readers eyewitness views of the life and times of each individual covered in The Importance Of series.

Finally, each volume is enhanced by photographs, bibliographies, chronologies, and comprehensive indexes. For both the casual reader and the student engaged in research, The Importance Of biographies will be a fascinating adventure into the lives of people who have helped shape humanity's past, present, and will continue to shape its future.

The Great Adventure

The name Napoleon Bonaparte brings forth an image of military conquest. At the beginning of the nineteenth century, he was considered the greatest soldier of his time by most people and the greatest of all time by many. He used his almost magical skills to win victory after victory for France and to carve out the largest and wealthiest empire the world had seen since the fall of Rome. In almost two centuries since his last victory, his reputation for strategic brilliance, indomitable courage, and inspired leadership has continued in the face of even bloodier and more wide-ranging wars than he him-

Jacques Louis David's painting of Napoleon leading his troops across the Alps. Names carved in stones at lower left hint that David believed Napoleon's greatness compared with that of famed warrior-rulers Hannibal and Charlemagne.

self had ever conceived. To be mentioned in the same breath with Napoleon is the supreme compliment to any general.

Yet, for all his military genius, Napoleon is not universally honored as a leader today. His triumphs involved the slaughter of millions. He enriched France by literally stealing the treasures of other lands. He spoke grandiosely of spreading freedom while enslaving a continent. He brought great glory to France, yet also great hardship. And, when he finally fell from power, his country's borders were less extensive than they had been when he first took command.

For every historian who honors Napoleon's name, another equally qualified expert finds him a blot on humanity's history. No doubt there was greatness in the man, but whether he used it more for good or for evil may never be settled.

That, however, is a moral question. All observers agree that Napoleon Bonaparte was one of the most important shapers of the modern world. His contributions to military science are unquestioned, of course. His Code Napoleon is the basis of law in France and much of Europe today. His centralization of France's government has been the model for countless dictatorships. His foreign policies led directly to the creation of the modern European states of Italy, Germany, and Poland and to the expansion of the United States from a tiny collection of former colonies into the most powerful nation on earth. The French Revolution's ideals of liberty, equality, and brotherhood, which he took care to export, became the catalyst for nationalistic movements that have dominated politics in the past two centuries.

Most of the changes Napoleon wrought were unforeseen by the general himself, of

The French Revolution was one of history's bloodiest wars. Yet its ideals of liberty, equality, and fraternity inspire nations to this day.

course. He set events in motion. He was the mover. Where it would all end was beyond any person's ability to divine. Perhaps this is his strongest appeal: he cast the dice and let his fate ride on the roll. His rise to the heights was a great adventure. "My maxim was," he said, "*la carriére est ouverte aux talents*—without distinction of birth or fortune."[1] Lacking both as starting points, he nevertheless became for a time the most powerful individual on the face of the earth. Perhaps never before or since has the world seen such a volatile mixture of undeniable ability combined with unbridled ambition, sustained energy,

Sculptor Vincenzo Vela's statue The Last Days of Napoleon *depicts the exiled emperor, sick at heart and in body, broken by the loss of his most cherished possession—power.*

supreme opportunism, and unflagging courage. He took audacious risks to achieve his ends, yet had the nerve and will to carry them through. Nothing was beyond his reach. "You write to me that it's impossible," he told one of his generals. "The word is not French."[2]

Ultimately, he fell. And he descended much further than if he had been cut down by a sniper's bullet in battle (an ending he no doubt would have preferred). His lot was to face imprisonment—shorn of all his honors and titles. Worst of all, shorn of any power to change his world. No other ending could have been worse for him. No other ending could have done justice to his story.

As he himself once said, "I . . . love power. I love it as a musician loves his violin."[3]

Chapter

1 An Emperor and a King

December 2, 1804, dawned cold in Paris with the tart scent of promised snow in the air. But the frigid temperature could not keep excited crowds from flooding the streets to gawk at the renowned and bejeweled dignitaries gathered in the city that day. At nine in the morning, a dozen glitter-

Napoleon—emperor of France at thirty-five. Despite a revolution to replace the tyranny of royalty with the rule of the people, France soon gave Napoleon absolute power.

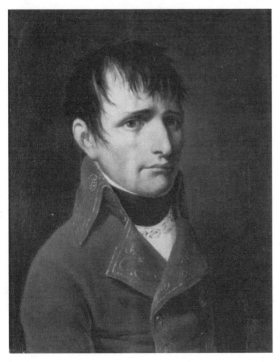

ing processions—representatives from various cities and administrative arms of the realm—began making their way through the streets. Each caravan was near bursting with stout horses, ornate carriages, elegantly clad servants, shining soldiers, and many of the most famous and powerful men of France, accompanied by their beautiful women. The processions traveled at a stately pace from various parts of the city to Notre Dame Cathedral where an event unthinkable only a few years before was about to unfold. With Pope Pius VII presiding, Napoleon Bonaparte would be crowned emperor of France.

Napoleon himself arrived at Notre Dame in a carriage emblazoned with a huge purple "N." It took more than an hour for the entourage in his parade of accompanying carriages to find their places in the cathedral.

At a mere thirty-five years of age, General Bonaparte already ruled unchallenged over France, his word literally law. He was "First Consul for Life"—dictator as long as he lived—of what was still referred to as the French "Republic," and he was slipping comfortably into the habits of royalty. More and more in his conversations, the people of France ceased to be "citizens" and became instead "my subjects," a truer designation of his relationship with the

The guillotine, a French invention, came to symbolize the horrors unleashed during the Reign of Terror. The guillotine was used often during this terrible time.

Less than a dozen years before, the beheading by guillotine of Louis XVI brought a shocking, sudden, and complete end to more than 900 years of monarchy in France. Then the cry had been "Liberty, Equality, and Brotherhood," but the Revolution, which had proclaimed a new freedom for all had turned viciously on itself. Thousands had been executed because they were thought to be against the Revolution or only lukewarm in their enthusiasm—or simply because someone in power wanted them eliminated. Even most of the revolutionary leaders responsible for ending the *ancien régime* had themselves become victims of "Madame Guillotine." The blade fell time and again until few felt free and even fewer felt safe. The glorious French Revolution became the Reign of Terror. And, when the blood lust was finally satisfied, the new government proved too weak, too divided, too confused to save France.

Then, just as all seem destined to be lost in a sea of chaos, there arose—almost from nowhere—this new Moses. He promised to restore order, reinstitute law, tame the extremists, inspire the masses, and lead France to ever greater victories on the battlefield. If there were those in the crowd that lined the Paris streets that cold December day who questioned the proceeding and felt the Revolution had been betrayed by the dictatorship of this single, all-powerful, and now *royal* Bonaparte, their cries of caution were drowned by the cheers of the mob. A carefully managed national election had voted 3,572,329 to 2,569 to establish a monarchy with Napoleon Bonaparte at its head. Most of the French were more than happy to exchange their shaky freedom for order, prosperity, and triumph. The former lead-

people. He had begun to sign routine proclamations and official letters with only his first name or often only "N," just as French kings in preceding centuries had signed "Louis" or "L." Now, with his ascendance to the imperial rank, the First Consul's absolute power was to be given the legitimacy and permanence of hereditary royalty.

ers of the Revolution who retained their heads were at least satisfied that a Napoleon on the throne made it impossible for the Bourbons to return to power—the monarchy, which had been in Bourbon hands for centuries was still hated. Foreign leaders, many of whom had fought against Napoleon's army to their regret, could convince themselves that Napoleon would be content to see peace restored to Europe.

More than 8,000 French and foreign dignitaries crowded into Notre Dame to witness the coronation. Napoleon sat on a golden throne, arrayed in a gold and ermine robe and wearing a small crown of golden laurel leaves, in his hand a sword supposedly carried by Charlemagne a thousand years before as Holy Roman Emperor. Five steps below Napoleon on a smaller throne sat Josephine, the empress-to-be, resplendent in diamonds and looking, according to reports, at least a dozen years younger than her actual age of forty-one.

Pope Pius VII was also present for the coronation. Although the Revolution had made a vain attempt to outlaw religion, and the Church had indeed lost much of its prerevolutionary influence and prestige, France remained almost entirely Roman Catholic. Some of the pope's cardinals had denounced the proposed crowning of the "upstart" Napoleon as sacrilege and urged the pontiff to remain in Rome. The pope, however, was a practical man, who believed that his participation in the coronation might influence Napoleon to restore Roman Catholicism to its traditional seat of power in France. At the very least, the new emperor might be induced to return several papal territories to the Vatican. To smooth his way toward asking these favors, Pius, since his arrival in Paris

On Guard for the Future

Although Napoleon's extreme ambition was certainly enough to lead him to become emperor, American historian Edward Mc-Nall Burns, in Western Civilizations, *points out a practical reason.*

"His action [in making himself emperor] was influenced partly by the growth of opposition. Several attempts had recently been made to take his life, and royalist plots were being hatched against him. Napoleon proceeded against the conspirators with characteristic ruthlessness. Scores were arrested upon mere suspicion, and some of the most prominent were singled out for execution. Having thus disposed of his chief enemies, Napoleon evidently concluded that the best way to guard against future trouble would be to establish a dynasty of his own and thereby cut the ground from under all Bourbon pretenders."

a week before, had been the soul of agreeability. When Josephine confided that she and Napoleon had been wed in a civil ceremony, Pius VII happily remarried them in the sight of God three days before the coronation.

For his part, Napoleon gave the pope "every courtesy except deference; the Emperor was not to be awed into admitting any superior power."[4]

The coronation ceremony began with Pius VII ascending to the altar. Napoleon and Josephine knelt before him and were anointed with the sacred oil of royal France. In reality, it was not the same oil that had been used to install generations of Bourbons. That had been publicly burned a half-dozen years earlier at the suggestion of the zealous Alexandre de Beauharnais, one of the leaders of the Revolution and, ironically, Josephine's first husband.

Then Napoleon descended the steps to meet General Kellerman, who stood holding the crown on a tray. What happened next shocked many in the cathedral, who had expected to see the pope crown Napoleon. Instead, the new emperor lifted the crown and placed it on his own head,

Boomerang

Arnold Toynbee, perhaps the twentieth century's most honored historian, argued in A Study of History *that Napoleon's use of Pius VII in his coronation ultimately did the emperor more harm than good.*

"Napoleon's mistake was to summon the pope from Rome to Paris to assist at his coronation as Emperor of a reconstituted substitute for the Holy Roman Empire; and, by flouting Rome and bullying her sovereign pontiff, he won, not respect for his own political power, but sympathy for the helplessness of his venerable victim."

Pope Pius VII became Napoleon's puppet.

Napoleon's coronation as emperor in 1804 recalled the days of Charlemagne's Holy Roman Empire—with one significant difference: The emperor crowned himself. By this action, Napoleon made it clear that his authority would not be subject to the Church.

crowning himself. Napoleon had arranged this turn of events with the amiable Pius before the ceremony. Napoleon's act allowed him to receive the blessing of the pope, the leader of Roman Catholicism, without giving the appearance of being in any way subject to the pope's commands. He was a self-made emperor.

As emperor, he crowned Josephine empress with a tiara of diamonds. Pius VII kissed him on the cheek and intoned, *"Vivat imperator in aeternum"* ("Long live the emperor"). After the pope sang mass, the emperor placed his hand on the Gospels and recited his oath of office.

By three o'clock, the ceremony was complete. Snow was falling on Paris. Napoleon turned to Joseph, his brother. "If only our father could see us now," he said.[5]

The First Stage of the Revolution, 1789–1792

But before all this happened, before Napoleon could become emperor, massive historical changes had to have taken place. As the eighteenth century approached its final decade, France was the idol of Europe.

King Louis XVI was absolute ruler over France in the late eighteenth century when his court, his queen, and his realm were the envy of Europe. His inept rule, however, eventually led to his overthrow and execution.

A powerful nation with a population of 25 million—the largest in Europe—and a strong army, its capital Paris was the cultural center of the continent. All over Europe, educated people spoke French, copied French fashions and customs, and did their best to *be* French. King Louis XVI was the most envied of monarchs; his beautiful queen, Marie Antoinette, the embodiment of royalty. Of all the nations in the world, France seemed the most secure against revolution.

But beneath the sparkling surface, France had many problems that would lead it to the bloodiest revolution the world had yet seen. France was like a glorious red apple that is rotten at the core.

The king of France, Louis XVI, ruled, according to the theory that had prevailed for centuries, that is, by *divine right*, the belief that God himself recognized him as the leader of the nation. In theory, the king held absolute power. But Louis was weak, easily swayed, and actually rather stupid. He had never wanted to rule. The nobles at his court, led by his spendthrift wife, Marie Antoinette, had little trouble in getting their own way whenever a decision had to be made. "The king is not a coward. He possesses an abundance of passive courage, but he is overwhelmed by an awkward shyness and mistrust of himself," the queen explained. "He is afraid to command."[6]

The queen, who had come to Louis as an Austrian princess and whom he loved dearly, had no such problem. But her judgment was bad and her ability to empathize with anyone not of her station far worse than the king's. At first quite popular, she eventually became the detested symbol of the nobility's disdain for the common people. A famous story of the day had Marie Antoinette being told that the common people had no bread to eat. "Well," she is said to have responded, "let them eat cake." That she ever really said this is highly unlikely, but the story illustrates how little the nobility of France—and especially the queen—understood the ordinary French people.

It was important for people to believe that their leaders had some understanding and concern for them. France was far from a modern unified nation. The people thought of themselves less as "French" than as subjects of the king of France. The

Marie Antoinette, flanked by her husband, holds court. As queen, Marie Antoinette made numerous state decisions. Unfortunately, her judgment was poor and her concern for her subjects almost nonexistent. The people later repaid her insensitivity by sending her to the guillotine.

distinction, though it might appear slight, went to the root of the people's loyalty. In a war, for example, soldiers fought for their king, not for their country. They had no stake, other than surviving, in the outcome. Nationalism, the personal involvement of citizens in the advancement of their country's fortunes, was unknown in most European countries. England, where the king ruled under limits imposed by an elected parliament, was the exception. Each Englishman had a personal interest in his nation's welfare, an attitude the French had yet to acquire. When a strong, effective king ruled France, the people's loyalty to him was sufficient to keep them generally satisfied. But Louis XVI was neither strong nor effective.

The people of France were divided into three *estates* or classes: the clergy, the nobles, and everyone else—peasants, city workers, and middle class. Taken together, the first two estates, the clergy and nobles, accounted for about 2 percent of the population. Yet they held most of the wealth and all the power.

The First Estate, the clergy in this almost completely Roman Catholic country, had two faces. On one hand were the humble parish priests, hardworking and devout, who usually tried their best to improve the lot of the common people. But the higher offices of the church—archbishops, bishops, and abbots—were open only to members of the nobility. Many of these ecclesiastical officials lived lives of showy luxury while displaying little interest in their religious duties. With the national treasury nearly empty, the Church enjoyed an annual income that amounted, in today's money, to $200 million. The clergy paid only nominal taxes on its vast holdings; the nobles paid nothing.

The Second Estate, the nobility, held all the high government offices. In many cases, Louis had sold the posts to wealthy nobles to raise money. Often, an office-holder did nothing but collect his salary and bribes; others were so unsuited to their positions that they might better have "done nothing." Although the terrible level of incompetence paralyzed institutions and increased debt, the king could not take back the offices without returning the money that had bought them. Many nobles owned huge estates supported by peasants who paid manorial dues in the form of produce, labor, and money. While the landed nobles who lived on their great estates contributed nothing to the support of the realm, the nobles at the court of Louis XVI were even worse. Their idle lives turned on elegant fashions, elaborate banquets, and gifts from the king.

The cost of supporting the nation fell almost completely to the Third Estate, particularly to the peasants, those with the least to give. Meanwhile, a series of wars conducted by Louis XVI's grandfather had greatly depleted the government's wealth. Ironically, aid given to the American revolutionaries in hope of injuring England during the American War for Independence had just about wiped out the treasury. As a result, Louis XVI was forced to borrow money. Soon, merely paying the interest on his loans took more than half of what taxation brought in. France was in the curious position of being a prosperous nation that was nearly bankrupt. Had the king been a strong leader, he might have forced his nobles to pay their fair share. But Louis was never one to face up to a crisis. And then he made a fatal mistake. Hoping to find new revenue, he convened

The storming of the Bastille. The attack on the old fortress prison on July 14, 1789, by a mob of armed French commoners was a turning point in French history. It sparked an armed revolution that would overthrow the government.

the Estates General, a parliament made up of representatives of the three estates; it had not met since 1614.

On May 5, 1789, the Estates General met in Paris. Traditionally, each of the three parts of the Estates General voted in a bloc, assuring the clergy and nobles of a two-to-one victory margin on any question. The Third Estate outnumbered the first two, however, and insisted on a one-man, one-vote format. When the nobles and clergy refused, the Third Estate stomped out of the meeting hall and reassembled at a nearby tennis court.

The representatives of the Third Estate belonged primarily to the middle class, or bourgeoisie: merchants, lawyers, bankers, doctors, and professors. Many were wealthy and successful within the limits possible under Louis XVI, but they were hardly content. They demanded that the government stop interfering in business, end censorship whereby criticism of the government could land a man in prison, and wipe out the privileges of the nobility that kept the bourgeoisie from holding high offices. In short, they wanted equality. They proposed limiting the power of the king and creating a written constitution.

The nobles and most of the clergy refused to join the Estates General. In June the representatives of the Third Estate declared themselves the National Assembly and claimed that they represented the entire nation.

Too late, Louis XVI tried to close down the National Assembly, ordering it to disperse. "We are here by the will of the people," shouted one representative. "We will go only if we are driven out by the point of a bayonet."[7] The king backed down.

Nevertheless, Louis and the nobles continued to oppose the Assembly. Armed troops gathered outside Paris, awaiting the king's word. But, by now, the scent of freedom pervaded Paris. The common people armed themselves to oppose the troops. On July 14, 1789, they attacked the Bastille, a huge old fortress infamous for housing political prisoners. Many of the soldiers stationed there were slaughtered, the governor of the prison was beheaded, and the prisoners were freed.

Upon hearing of the event, Louis exclaimed, "Why that is a revolt!" This observation was corrected by a member of the court nobility: "No, Sire, it is a revolution!"[8] Actually they were both wrong. The Revolution had begun when the Third Estate took control of the Estates General; the fall of the Bastille is more properly classified as a riot. Regardless, it saved the Revolution.

Badly shaken, Louis ordered his army to return to their posts outside the city rather than risk further confrontations, and many of his nobles began leaving the country in panic. Today in France, Bastille Day is celebrated much as Americans celebrate Independence Day.

But the storming of the Bastille signified that the mob would play an increasing role in the Revolution, and with the mob came violence. In October, a Paris crowd of 20,000, made up mostly of women demanding bread, invaded the palace at Versailles, twelve miles outside the city. They killed two guards and confronted the king. Humiliated, Louis was forced to return to Paris, where he could be protected by the National Assembly. At the same time, peasants all over France rose up against their oppressors. Terrified that the nobles would return to power and wreak revenge, peas-

Peasants armed with farm implements go on a rampage in 1789. One mob, 20,000 strong and composed mostly of women, stormed the royal palace at Versailles and confronted King Louis. All over France, peasant mobs rebelled violently against the aristocracy.

ant mobs looted and burned manors, destroyed tax records, and in some cases lynched nobles.

Meanwhile, the National Assembly went on with its work. Many nobles, at last realizing that the old ways were gone forever, renounced their special privileges and joined the Assembly. Influential in the thinking of the representatives were the works of the *philosophes,* eighteenth-century writers who had begun to look at government in a new way—not as a burden imposed by divine right on people but as the servant of society, deriving its power from the will of the people. It was this line of thinking that led Thomas Jefferson to write in the American *Declaration of Independence:*

> We hold these truths to be self-evident; that all men are created equal; that they are endowed by their creator with certain unalienable rights; that among these are life, liberty, and the pursuit of happiness; that to secure these rights, governments are instituted among men, deriving their just powers from the consent of the governed.

In August 1789, the National Assembly issued the *Declaration of the Rights of Man and of Citizens,* a landmark in the history of liberty. Among other rights, it guaranteed the presumption of innocence under law, protected private property, and abolished censorship. It defined liberty as "the power to do anything that does not injure others." Perhaps most revolutionary of all was the opening sentence: "Men are born free and remain free and equal in rights." With a stroke of a pen, all the ancient privileges of the nobility had ceased to exist.

The Assembly revised the justice system, outlawed censorship, and eased restrictions on business. It also sharply

This depiction of the Declaration of the Rights of Man and of Citizens *shows that, like the king's right to rule, his subjects' human rights also came from God.*

limited the power of the clergy, in effect placing the Church under state control. In 1791 a constitution was finally drafted and passed. It was essentially a conservative document, limiting the powers of the king, establishing a legislature, and giving the vote only to men who owned property. In September, Louis XVI accepted it. He had no choice; by then, the king was a prisoner.

Although the king had seemed to go along with the work of the Assembly, in reality, he hoped to be restored as absolute monarch. He encouraged pockets of resistance within France, secretly contacted nobles who had escaped the country, and sought to raise an army to topple the Revolution. On the night of June 20, 1791, he and his family took flight for the border. There he planned to join regiments loyal to him and then convince other European monarchs to join him in a counterrevolution.

But the royal family was captured, the plan exposed, and the king's household sent back to Paris. Until then, the French people had been generally forgiving of their king, viewing him more as a victim of bad advice from those around him than as the perpetrator of their woes. But with the news that Louis had planned to lead a foreign army against his own subjects, the people turned on him. He was a traitor.

The first stage of the French Revolution ended. Its second and far bloodier stage was about to begin.

2 For Patriotism

Napoleon's rise from obscure army officer to emperor of France in less than ten years was, to say the least, rapid. All the more so considering that in the eyes of many of his subjects, he was not truly French. There were always many in the realm who referred to him as "the Corsican." Not to his face, of course; Napoleon hated the name.

The fourth largest island in the Mediterranean Sea, Corsica—about the size of the state of Louisiana—nestles just north of its bigger sister Sardinia in the nook created by the intersection of France's southern coast and Italy's eastern shore. Since Roman times, Corsica had been owned by one European power or another. From the fourteenth century, the Italian city of Genoa had controlled its fate, but in 1768, after a series of revolts made Corsica more trouble than the Genoese felt it was worth, the turbulent little island was sold to France.

Small farms flourish in Corsica's many fertile valleys, but the island's wild, mountainous landscape lends itself best to the raising of sheep. "The people," wrote the Roman historian Livy, "resemble their country, being as ungovernable as wild beasts."[9] By the eighteenth century, most Europeans still considered the Corsican people a wild and unruly lot. With a limited economy, few Corsicans achieved the

prosperity necessary to furnish their children with a first-rate education. The Buonapartes (the original spelling of the family name) were numbered among the island's

The island of Corsica, off Italy's west coast, belonged to France when Napoleon was born there in 1769. Thus he was a French subject, but not of French blood.

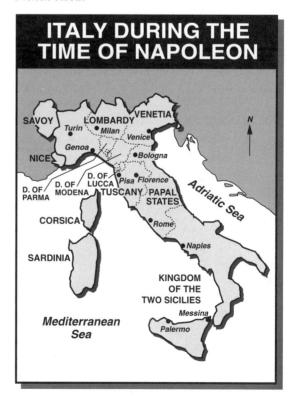

ITALY DURING THE TIME OF NAPOLEON

SAVOY
LOMBARDY
VENETIA
Turin
Milan
Venice
Genoa
Bologna
NICE
D. OF LUCCA
Pisa Florence
D. OF PARMA
D. OF MODENA
TUSCANY
PAPAL STATES
Adriatic Sea
CORSICA
Rome
SARDINIA
Naples
KINGDOM OF THE TWO SICILIES
Messina
Mediterranean Sea
Palermo
N

Napoleon's father, Carlo Maria Buonaparte, was a lawyer and a member of the lesser nobility of Corsica. He served in the Franco-Corsican administration of the island.

petty nobility, a distinction that earned local respect but little wealth. Carlo Maria Buonaparte (1746–1785), Napoleon's father, was a rural lawyer and notary. Such clients as he had were more likely to pay for his services in wool or lambs than in coin.

On August 15, 1769, in the village of Ajaccio, Napoleone (again the original spelling) was born the fourth child and second son of Carlo and Letizia Ramolino (1750–1836) de Buonaparte. Only two months before, France had landed soldiers on Corsica to suppress yet another uprising. "I was born," he wrote twenty years later, "when my country was dying. Thirty thousand Frenchmen disgorged upon our shores, drowning the throne of liberty in a sea of blood; such was the hateful spectacle that offended my infant eyes."[10] Nevertheless, by entering this world shortly after the sale of the island to France had been "finalized," Napoleone was technically a French citizen.

The Buonapartes were followers of Pasquale di Paoli (1725–1807), the leader of the Corsican movement for independence. Letizia, not yet twenty, shared the hard life of a revolutionary with her husband while carrying their son, enduring primitive camps, narrow escapes, forced marches, and limited rations. Sometimes they were compelled to hide out in caves.

Letizia Buonaparte, Napoleon's mother. When Napoleon was born, she and her husband lived like soldiers in the camp of a Corsican freedom fighter who opposed French rule.

Although undoubtedly sincere in his pursuit of Corsican liberty, Carlo also had an opportunistic streak. He treasured his noble pedigree, however minor, and saw in it a way to advance his standing with the French. After all, his family was growing and would continue to expand. All told, Carlo and Letizia would have thirteen children, eight of whom survived infancy: Joseph (1768–1844) was the oldest; Napoleone second. After him came Lucien (1775–1840), Maria Anna Elisa (1777–1820), Louis (1778–1846), Pauline (1780–1825), Maria Carolina (1782–1839), and Jerome (1784–1860). Thinking of his family's future, Carlo abandoned his revolutionary ways, made peace with France, and served in the Franco-Corsican administration of the island. The Buonapartes prospered.

Napoleon's opportunism—perhaps his dominant trait—might be traced genetically to his father; but in more ways, he resembled his mother. He said, "It is to my mother and her excellent principles that I owe all my success, and any good that I have done. I do not hesitate to affirm that the future of the child depends on its mother."[11] Letizia, he believed, was the source of his energy, courage, determination, and family loyalty.

Be that as it may, it was Carlo who was able to pull enough strings to secure Napoleone a place at the preparatory school at Autun in 1878. There, if legend is to be believed, the nine-year-old Corsican was bullied and laughed at by classmates who made fun of his accent and his small size. What is known for certain is that at Autun the boy gained a knowledge of the French language and discarded the final "e" of his Christian name. After only a few months, Carlo managed to have his

Young Napoleon and his mother. Napoleon credited his mother as the source of his energy, courage, determination, and family loyalty as well as his later success.

tenuous claim of nobility recognized at the French royal court. This led to an appointment on scholarship for young Napoleon to the more distinguished military academy at Brienne-le-Château in eastern France. "It was the cardinal event in the boy's life, for it destined him to a martial career, and—almost to the end—to think of life and destiny in terms of war."[12]

Apparently Napoleon was an erratic student, excellent in mathematics, less so in history, weak in "accomplishments"—music, dancing, and social skills. It's clear that he preferred reading in his room to carousing with his fellow students. After five years at Brienne, he received a final report: "This boy would make an excellent sailor."[13] But

Napoleon in all his life was never much interested in naval affairs. Even when his success in land battles depended on some intricacy at sea, he cared only for results. To the fifteen-year-old, there was no question where his military future lay. The navy had always been the lesser wing of France's armed forces. Glory and advancement resided in the army. In 1784 he was one of the students chosen from the country's twelve military academies to receive advanced instruction at France's leading military college, the École Militaire in Paris.

It took Napoleon a year to complete his studies, about half the time most students needed. At sixteen, he was commissioned a second lieutenant in the artillery. His choice of branch was to prove significant. Among the French officer corps—all sons of nobility—the cavalry retained the most prestige, based on sound seventeenth-century principles of warfare. But much had changed during the eighteenth century, and it was the artillery that was the main recipient of the technical improvements of the time.

When young Napoleon Bonaparte became a second lieutenant in the artillery in 1785, the life of a French army officer was leisurely. With no war under way, the

Students at Brienne-le-Château military school make fun of Napoleon's small stature and his Corsican accent. Military school set Napoleon on a path that taught him to view life and destiny in terms of war. He kept this view for the rest of his life.

Napoleon as Werther

In this excerpt from the Durants' Age of Napoleon, *the young Napoleon reveals his "Werther-esque" side.*

"Always alone in the midst of men, I come to my room to dream by myself, to abandon myself to my melancholy in all its sharpness. In which direction does it lead today? Toward death. . . . What fury drives me to my own destruction? Indeed, what am I to do in this world? Since die I must, is it not just as well to kill myself?"

Napoleon was often melancholy and brooding as a youth.

routine of base life was decidedly undemanding: occasional drills, sporadic inspections, frequent parties and dances. Fortunately for the young Napoleon, who was ill at ease at festive events, long leaves were easy to get. He spent nearly a year and a half back in Corsica where, among other things, he began to write a history of his native island.

Carlo Buonaparte died of a gastric ulcer in 1785, but his son Joseph, the oldest male, had not yet found a place in the world. Napoleon then became the family breadwinner, supporting his mother and seven siblings on his meager second lieutenant's pay. That he had little money left for entertainment may have been the source of some of his isolation, but he also enjoyed thinking of himself as a loner. A popular book of the day was *The Sorrows of Young Werther,* Goethe's dreary narrative in which the gloomy, misunderstood young hero rejects the world and kills himself. Napoleon read it several times.

By the time he turned twenty, life looked a lot better, as it almost always does. He became more at ease in social situations, though never the life of any party. He discovered the charms of women. And the world was changing in Paris.

Although his family had its slight claim to nobility, the young Napoleon was middle class in his thinking and found no problem in embracing the aims of the Revolution when it began. Moreover, he saw in it a way for Corsica to achieve freedom from France, and he envisioned himself as playing a leading role in his native land. He was one of the Corsicans who succeeded in getting the National Assembly in Paris to accept some reforms that gave Corsica a degree of self-government. Resigning his commission in the French artillery, he became a lieutenant colonel in the Corsican National Guard. But, he was not completely trusted by the sixty-five-year-old Paoli, who headed the island regime. Apparently, Napoleon, who had been "too Corsican" for the French, had become "too French" for the Corsicans.

The Second French Revolution, 1792

By the spring of 1792, the radicals called *Jacobins* were gaining influence in the Assembly in Paris. Instead of working for reform with the monarchy, they wanted to take the Revolution still further, to arrive at a complete republic with no king at all. They promised to empower every French citizen in absolute equality. The backing of the Paris mob gave the radicals some advantage because the threat of violence lurked behind their calls for legislative action.

Despite the growing power of the Jacobins, a more conservative group, the

The Jacobins were a radical faction in the French National Assembly. They advocated a republican style of government in which there would be no king.

Girondins, still held the upper hand. They advocated war with France's foreign enemies. The Girondins had a number of reasons for going to war. Some, who had interests in armaments and shipping, simply thought war would be good for business, but most held more patriotic motives. Support for the Revolution and the new constitution was far from unanimous in France; some believed that war would unite the country, with all Frenchmen answering the call against an outside foe. At the other extreme, some of the Jacobins feared that their side might be weakened if their back-ers were distracted by war. Surprisingly, most Jacobins also favored war. Many on both sides believed that other European monarchs were preparing to invade France and return Louis XVI to his seat of absolute authority; it was important, they thought, to beat the enemy to the punch, to strike before the counterrevolutionaries were at full strength. Many radical Jacobins saw in war a way to spread the Revolution to all of Europe; they would be satisfied only when every government on the continent was a republic.

Ironically, the counterrevolutionaries in France also favored war. Many military leaders thought that war would so strengthen the army that it would be able to place Louis back on his throne even though two-thirds of the officers were in exile.

On April 20, 1792, France declared war on Austria.

Inexperienced French soldiers led by inexperienced officers proved no match for the Austrian army. The war went badly. Prussia joined Austria and together they

The Image of History

The famous historian Thomas Carlyle published his history entitled The French Revolution *in 1837. His style, though at times difficult, seeks to put readers in the action by bombarding them with short, vivid images. Here is a sample from his account of the fall of the Bastille.*

"Let conflagration rage; of whatsoever is combustible! Guard-rooms are burnt, *Invalides* mess-rooms. A distracted *'perukemaker* [a wig maker] with two fiery torches' is for burning 'the saltpetres of the Arsenal';—had not a woman run screaming; had not a Patriot, with some tincture of *Natural Philosophy* [humanity], instantly struck the wind out of him (butt of musket on pit of stomach), overturned barrels, and stayed the devouring element. A young beautiful lady, seized escaping in these Outer Courts, and thought falsely to be *De Launay's* [the commander of the Bastille] daughter, shall be burnt in De Launay's sight; she lies swooned on a paillasse [a straw mattress]; but again a Patriot, it is brave Aubin Bonnemere the old soldier, dashes in, and rescues her. Straw is burnt; three cartloads of it, hauled thither, go up in white smoke: almost to the choking of Patriotism itself; so that Elie had, with singed brows, to drag back one cart; and Reole the 'gigantic haberdasher' another. Smoke as of *Tophet* [hell]; confusion as of Babel; noise as of the Crack of Doom! Blood flows; the *aliment* [nourishment] of new madness."

The executioner displays the severed head of King Louis XVI to a cheering crowd. Louis, whose power had been greatly reduced by the revolution, was arrested in 1792 when the radical Jacobins seized power in the National Assembly.

invaded France, pushing back the borders. The duke of Brunswick, the commander of the invading army, announced that Paris would be destroyed if the French did not restore Louis to his throne. In effect, he sealed Louis's fate.

The people of Paris reacted hysterically to the duke's threat. They stormed into the king's Paris palace and killed more than a hundred of his guards. Meanwhile, defeats on the battlefield brought the radical Jacobins to power in the Assembly. Six weeks after the invasion of his palace, Louis was arrested and tried before the Assembly as a traitor. He was accused of encouraging foreign troops to invade France, even though it was the Assembly itself that had declared war.

There was never a question that Louis would be found guilty. Conservatives favored exile or imprisonment as punishment, but the radicals realized that a living king would be a constant rallying point for counterrevolutionaries. They demanded and received the death penalty for Louis. On January 21, 1793, the doomed king mounted the thirteen steps of the scaffold to the guillotine.

At his execution, he showed more courage than he had ever exhibited while he reigned. "Frenchmen," he told the crowd, "I die innocent; it is from the scaffold and near to appearing before God that I tell you so. I pardon my enemies. I desire that France—"[14] A drum roll drowned out his final words.

Napoleon in Corsica

Napoleon spent most of the first four years of the Revolution in Corsica, but on trips to Paris, he witnessed some of the riots. He was far too much the opportunist to speak his mind openly at this point, preferring to wait to see which way the final wind would blow. His guarded tone in letters home exasperated his hot-headed younger brother Lucien, who wrote to Joseph:

> I believe that a man should place himself above circumstances and commit himself to a definite choice if he wants to be something and make a name for himself. The most hated men in history are those who sail according to the wind. . . . I have always been aware of a completely selfish ambition in Napoleone. . . . He seems to me to have the potentialities of a tyrant and I believe that he would be one if he were a king, and that his name would be held in horror by posterity.[15]

Even before Napoleon's rise to power, his younger brother Lucien keenly perceived a selfish ambition in Napoleon. Lucien predicted that his older brother, if ever a king, would be a tyrant dishonored by history.

Fighting Words

One of the legislators who saw warfare as a way of exporting the Revolution is quoted by Marvin Perry in Man's Unfinished Journey.

"Let us say to [other nations] that ten million Frenchmen, kindled by the fire of liberty, armed with the sword, with reason, with eloquence, would be able, if incensed, to change the face of the world and make the tyrants tremble on their thrones."

The Good Side

Historian Edward McNall Burns in Western Civilizations *explains that the legacy of the Reign of Terror was not totally bad for France.*

"Despite the violence of the Reign of Terror, the second stage of the French Revolution was marked by some worthy achievements. Such leaders as Robespierre, fanatical though they may have been, were nevertheless sincere humanitarians, and it was not to be expected that they would ignore the opportunity to inaugurate reforms. Among their most significant accomplishments were the aboliton of slavery in the colonies; the prohibition of imprisonment for debt; the establishment of the metric system of weights and measures; and the repeal of primogeniture, so that property might not be inherited exclusively by the oldest son but must be divided in substantially equal portions among all the immediate heirs."

Lucien was more than willing to commit himself to a definite choice. He chose to accuse Paoli of treason against the Revolution and succeeded in bringing the old Corsican leader to trial. Although evidence shows that Paoli hoped to bring Corsica into the war *against* France, evidence had ceased to matter in those times. The Paolists were in control of Corsica, however. The Bonapartes were defeated, and only by calling on ancient loyalties to the family were they able to escape the island.

By June 1793, Napoleon found himself banished from his place of birth, adrift without means. In Paris, the government was convulsed in a power struggle. In southern France where the Bonapartes landed, a civil war raged between the revolutionaries and the loyalists.

He was twenty-three years old; his prospects had never been bleaker. Yet, strange as it may seem, this dark and dangerous moment marked the beginning of the rise to power of Napoleon Bonaparte.

The Committee Takes Charge, 1793–1794

In 1793 the war continued to go badly. Although French troops were able to throw back the combined force of Austria and Prussia, that success only brought further opposition from elsewhere in Europe. Britain, Holland, Spain, Sardinia, and the German states joined Austria and Prussia in opposing France.

At the same time, resistance to the Revolution was growing within France. In the provinces, counterrevolutionaries tried to seize power. In Paris, riots over politics were replaced by riots over food.

To prosecute the war, the Jacobins created the Committee of Public Safety, and in this body, the real power lay. With a foreign army at the borders, the committee took control of every aspect of French life. Agents with soldiers were sent to other parts of the nation to ruthlessly combat loyalist outbreaks against the Revolution. The committee believed France would not be safe until all opposition to the Revolution was stamped out. They ordered members of the nobility arrested, then those who sympathized with the nobility, and soon those *suspected* of being in any way opposed to the Revolution. At their trials, if such the proceedings can be called, the accused were not allowed to present evidence in their defense. In effect, accusation became conviction. And conviction usually meant the guillotine. Thus began, for the most patriotic of reasons, the bloody period called the Reign of Terror.

Each day, as carts bearing the condemned rumbled through the streets of Paris, a great crowd assembled to cheer and jeer around the scaffold. One by one, the prisoners were strapped to a plank and placed beneath the guillotine blade. As the drums rolled and the blade fell, a great shout invariably arose among the bug-eyed spectators. Two men tossed the bodies into a waiting cart painted red. The

A cart carries members of the Girondins, the conservative group in the National Assembly, to the guillotine for execution during the Reign of Terror. Although the Girondins had engineered the revolution of 1789, they were later seen as a threat by the ruling faction of Jacobins.

An eighteenth-century caricature of the ruthless Robespierre squeezing the life's blood from a heart into his drinking goblet. Such satire would doubtless have earned the artist a rendezvous with the guillotine.

heads went into a second red cart. Women in the crowd wore miniature guillotines as jewelry. Children played with toy guillotines. It was a great show.

Marie Antoinette paid for her spendthrift ways with her head in October. Other nobles who had not had the good sense to get out of France followed her in death. Ironically, a few had actually favored the Revolution, but service to the cause brought no absolution for the sin of having noble blood. Soon the crowd stopped asking or caring whose time had come, mindful only of their daily amusement.

To consolidate its control, the Committee of Public Safety turned on the Girondins. The very men who had led the Revolution in its early days were condemned. Next, the members of the committee began to accuse one another of treason. Of all the members of the committee, Maximilien Robespierre was perhaps the most brilliant and certainly the most cold-blooded. He brought charges against all who stood in his way, eliminating them one by one, with the precision of a surgeon wielding a scalpel, as opposed to the shotgun approach of the mob. In June 1794, he forced through a decree that "established the death penalty for advocating monarchy or calumniating [slandering] the republic; for outraging morality; for giving out false news; for stealing public property; for profiteering or embezzling; for impeding the transport of food; for interfering in any way with the prosecution."[16] Armed with such a catch-all law to intimidate or destroy any who opposed him, Robespierre was the master of France.

Numbered among his followers was Napoleon Bonaparte.

3 Fortune's Favorite

As soon as he had his family safely removed to France, Napoleon sought to rejoin the French army. It was the only trade for which he was suited. With war raging both on the borders and in pockets of the counterrevolution within France itself, and with so many officers having fled the country, he was able to secure a commission as a captain in the artillery with almost ridiculous ease. The officer in charge in Nice was General du Teil, the brother of his former commander, who immediately dispatched Napoleon to bring back supplies from Avignon, 125 miles to the west. It turned out that Avignon was in the hands of counterrevolutionaries, so Napoleon joined the army of General Carteaux, which had been sent from Paris to quell the insurgents. He took an honorable if minor part in the recapture of Avignon, his first actual war experience.

Carteaux's army moved on to a siege of the strategic port city of Toulon in 1793. There, a mixed group of British, Spanish, and Italian troops and local royalist sympathizers controlled both the town and the arsenal. Whoever held Toulon dominated that part of the Mediterranean.

Shortly before the siege began, the commander of Carteaux's artillery, General Dommartin, was wounded in a minor action and had to be replaced. Accompanying Carteaux's army were several representatives of the Committee of Public Safety in Paris, sent to supervise the political operations. One of them, Antoine Christophe Saliceti, was a Corsican and old friend of the Bonapartes. He urged

Napoleon as a young officer. His rise through the ranks of the French army was meteoric—from captain to brigadier general—due to the favor of Robespierre and the Committee of Public Safety who ruled France.

Carteaux to place the twenty-four-year-old Napoleon in charge. Carteaux had more experienced artillery officers in his command, but he also knew his head would rest more securely on his neck if he listened to the representative from Paris.

Napoleon saw immediately that the key to Toulon was the fort overlooking the city. Its guns protected the harbor and allowed a British fleet to resupply the town with ease. If the fort could be overcome, the unprotected fleet would be forced to withdraw, and the town would fall. Somehow General Carteaux did not see it that way. Political expediency might force him to place this young captain in a position of apparent authority, but that did not mean

the general was ready to listen to the newcomer's schemes. The general believed the fort, called by some "Little Gibraltar," was too strong to be brought down by artillery. For three months, as Napoleon's frustration grew, General Carteaux's army was held at bay by the defenders of Toulon.

At last, Carteaux was replaced by General Dugommier, who recognized the merit of Napoleon's plan. In truth, it was a basic maneuver and might have been conceived by any experienced artilleryman. Given the green light, Napoleon moved his guns to a place he had discovered, where they could bombard the fort in relative safety. Within days, Napoleon's guns blew a hole in the fort's wall. A battalion of

French ships bombard the fort at Toulon.

French troops poured through and captured the bastion, then turned its cannon on the fleet in the harbor. The British set sail, burning the ships they could not save. Shorn of its supply ships, the city surrendered on December 19, 1793.

What followed was terrible: looting, raping, and mass executions. At one point, 200 French marines, who had been forced to heel to the counterrevolutionaries and had welcomed the French army as liberators, were lined up against a wall and shot without the hint of a trial. More formally, a guillotine was erected and kept busy—as many as 200 beheadings a day—in the center of town.

Although Napoleon apparently played no part in these outrages, he witnessed them, and they added to his growing cynicism. "Among so many conflicting ideas and so many perspectives, the honest man is confused and distressed and the skeptic becomes wicked," he wrote to Lucien. "Since one must take sides, one might as well choose the side that is victorious, the side which devastates, loots, and burns. Considering the alternative, it is better to eat than to be eaten."[17] Perhaps he was remembering Toulon on his deathbed, when he said, "In my youth I had illusions; I got rid of them fast."[18]

Regardless of the actions taken in the occupation of Toulon, the capture of the city was a personal triumph for Napoleon. His plan, obvious as it might have been, was given the lion's share of the credit for the success of the operation. Both General du Teil and Saliceti wrote to the minister of war in Paris lauding the young artillery captain. Even more important was the praise of Augustin Robespierre, brother of the man who was by then virtual dictator of France. Augustin, another representa-

Napoleon, imprisoned for ten days as a Robespierrist, studies his war charts as an official from the new French government enters the cell bearing a letter of pardon.

tive sent by the committee, described the "transcendent merit"[19] of Napoleon in a letter to Maximilien.

Within only a few months, the young captain was promoted—all the way to brigadier general!

Reversal of Fortune

By August, the new general was in prison awaiting trial and possible execution.

Napoleon had recognized that his sudden leap in rank was the result of his being favored by Robespierre and his followers. In the terminology of the day, he was a

Robespierre's arrest on July 27, 1794, brought the worst of the Reign of Terror to an end. He had sentenced thousands to die by the guillotine. Within a day of his arrest he himself met Madame Guillotine.

Robespierrist. Regardless of what he may have felt in his heart, he was perfectly willing to be identified with the rulers of France and to gain advantage from that position. But advantage existed only so long as Robespierre held power.

No man was more incorruptible than Maximilien Robespierre. Next to him, all others paled in their dedication to the Revolution. Too cold to be loved or even liked by the other revolutionary leaders, he was nevertheless respected and, as the executions grew in number and came closer to home, he was feared. At last, those who still had the power and courage to act turned on him. He was arrested, tried, and, on July 28, 1794, took his place beneath the guillotine.

With his death, the worst of the Reign of Terror ended. However, it was not for humane reasons that Robespierre fell, but simply another ruthless change at the top of government that saw a purge of the former leader and his followers, among them Napoleon. Fortunately for the young general, his association with the Robespierrists was not strong. He wrote an indignant letter to the new leaders in Paris, and his old admirer Saliceti interceded for him. After ten days, he was released from prison.

Although free, Napoleon was apparently still tarred with the Robespierrist brush; he found himself in a sort of limbo on inactive service at reduced pay. By May 1795, he was in Paris working in the planning section of the Committee of Public

Safety. It was a time for long walks, deep in thought and dreams, along the banks of the Seine. Many of his ambitious reveries were unrealistic, even a bit laughable. At one point, he considered going to Turkey, joining its army, and somehow carving himself an oriental kingdom out of the Middle East. Other dreams were more attainable. He had fallen in love.

Josephine de Beauharnais was one of the reigning queens of Parisian society, although her road to that position had been long, difficult, and at times dangerous. She was a creole—a person of French and Spanish descent—raised in relative luxury on the island of Martinique in the Caribbean. At the age of sixteen, she came to France, where she married Vicomte Alexandre de Beauharnais. Over the next few years, she bore him first a son, Eugene, and then a daughter, Hortense. When the Revolution arrived, de Beauharnais, though a nobleman, joined in enthusiastically and was one of its early leaders. And, along with so many of the early leaders, he eventually found his destiny beneath the blade of the guillotine. His widow was imprisoned for a time and threatened with the same fate, but eventually she was released and returned to Paris and its social whirl. There, by dint of her dark-haired beauty, lighthearted charm, and a strong practical streak, she achieved a position of prominence as one of the arbiters of Parisian fashion, taste, and manners.

Unfortunately, it was not a paid position. All the wealth of the vicomte de Beauharnais had been confiscated. When Josephine met General Bonaparte, she was being harried by armies of creditors. Under the mistaken impression that he was wealthy, she saw in Napoleon a way to pay off her many debts, but otherwise she was unimpressed at first. He was short, sallow, and retained his Corsican accent. Moreover, she quoted Shakespeare in describing him as having "a lean and hungry look."[20] The quotation was on the mark; in the original context of Shakespeare's play, those words brand a character dangerous.

Despite whatever reservations she may have had, Josephine sent her son Eugene to Napoleon to ask if he might aid her in recovering her late husband's sword. The ploy was as successful as it was transparent. The sword was returned and their relationship prospered.

Ironically, at first he thought *she* had money. As the main support of the entire Bonaparte family, he had to consider the practical side of any marriage. By marrying

Josephine de Beauharnais, shown here later as empress, was a widowed Paris socialite who at first courted Napoleon because she believed him to be wealthy.

Do as I Say, Not as . . .

Dale Carnegie is best known for his philosophy of winning friends and influencing people, but in an amusing book called Little Known Facts About Well-Known People, *he told this Napoleon story.*

"Napoleon had a veritable passion for always being on time. His motto was 'Time is everything,' and he once said, 'I may lose battles, but no one will ever see me lose minutes'; and yet he was two hours late for his own wedding [to Josephine]! The Justice of the Peace who was waiting to marry them got so tired that he yawned and fell asleep before Napoleon arrived."

The civil marriage of Napoleon and Josephine on March 9, 1796.

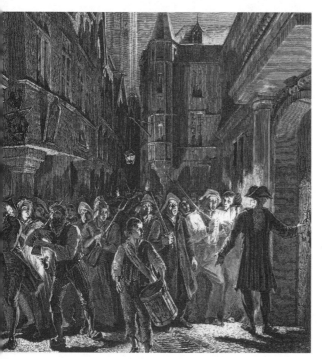

A mob of French peasants marches toward the National Convention in Paris. They planned to wrest power from the middle-class rulers, but Napoleon's troops stopped them.

Josephine, he stood to gain an entrance into Paris society that would surely advance his career as well as—he thought—a way to bring financial security to his mother, brothers, and sisters.

By the time Napoleon learned the truth of Josephine's finances, he was too deeply smitten to retreat. Their attraction for each other went beyond a mere exchange of—as it turned out, nonexistent—bank books. They really were in love, insofar as a widow with two children and a general with an insatiable ambition had room in their lives for true love.

Napoleon and Josephine were married in a civil ceremony on March 9, 1796. At thirty-three, she was six years older than

he. However, they brought the official account into closer accord with convention by fibbing on the license: she lowered her age to twenty-nine and he raised his to twenty-eight.

Defender of the Revolution

While Napoleon was conducting his romance with Josephine, his military career was rejuvenated by his once more being in the right place at the right time. Detractors might call him lucky, but until the end he had a marvelous ability to take full advantage of whatever circumstances presented themselves. In this case, another Paris riot was his opportunity.

The middle class, which had gained control at the beginning of the Revolution, had never released it. Even the most rabid of Jacobins, although they had the support of the volatile lower classes of Paris and profited by their occasional rioting, were steadfastly middle class. When Robespierre's puritanical middle-class regime was toppled, its replacement was simply another, slightly less brutal, wing of the bourgeoisie.

The new government, through a body called the National Convention, framed still another constitution. In this one the legislature was to consist of two chambers. But, instead of starting from scratch, the Convention stipulated that two-thirds of the new legislature be made up of representatives from the preceding National Assembly. By that clever maneuver, the middle class retained power firmly in their own hands.

The Paris mobs, which had been promised much but had seen mostly food shortages, inflationary prices, and hard times, rioted once more. And this time, they seemed fully intent on taking power themselves. They were joined by a still more dangerous force of royalists, aiming for the return of the monarchy. The entire Revolution was at risk. The commander of government troops in Paris ordered the advancing mob to disperse. When he was ignored, he shrugged and retreated.

Napoleon was at a theater when he heard about the new riots. He immediately went to the National Convention (merely out of curiosity, he later insisted) and found the legislators there in panic. The commander of government troops had been dismissed when he left the field to the rioters. A replacement was needed. Immediately!

Napoleon was spotted in the spectators' gallery, as surely he had intended, and his name was put forth for the command of the troops. The Convention assigned Paul Barras to organize the defense of the city and not incidentally of

Vicomte Paul Barras chose Napoleon to save the National Convention from the approaching mob. A wily political survivor, he had sided first with King Louis XVI, then Robespierre, then Napoleon, always managing to disassociate himself from each just before they fell from favor.

Robespierre's Goals

J. Christopher Herold in The Age of Napoleon *comments on the paradoxes of power and corruption.*

"As the revolution took its ever more violent course, the reformers were replaced by theorists, and the arch-theorist, Robespierre, gradually eliminated the others. His aim was to remake society. . . . Since men had become corrupted under the old order, the new order had to be imposed on them by a handful of incorruptible leaders who represented the 'general will'—that is, the will that the majority of the people should have had but had not."

their persons, in effect, asking him to name the military leader. He sent for Napoleon.

The general waited half an hour before accepting Barras's offer. He did not wish to appear too ready to take a command that was likely to result in the shedding of French blood by French weapons. However, in light of succeeding events, many historians suspect that Napoleon's delay may have been used to exact a promise of further promotion from Barras. Certainly Barras, who was first and foremost a survivor, was more than capable of entering into an agreement from which he himself was likely to benefit. By artfully choosing his friends and knowing exactly when to switch sides, Barras had more than once used the events of the time for personal advancement. A confidant of both Louis XVI and Robespierre, Barras had left their respective camps in time to profit by each man's death. His association with Napoleon was to redound to his benefit, and somehow, when a Bourbon monarchy was restored to the French throne in 1815, Barras was once more on the triumphant side. Displaying all the loyalty and morality of a scorpion, Barras was a schemer "whose appetite for beautiful women, beautiful young men, and money was the only wholesome trait in his character," as J. Christopher Herold describes him.[21]

By whatever promises were needed, Barras convinced Napoleon to take charge of defending the Convention against the mob. The next day, an estimated 25,000 angry Parisians advanced from two directions on the building housing the Convention. Napoleon, with fewer than 5,000 troops at his command, had anticipated the mob's routes and had his cannon at the ready. He ordered the insurgents to disperse. When his command was ignored, he ordered his artillery to fire point blank into the mob.

Some 200 to 300 besiegers were killed. Perhaps twice that many were wounded. The rest, thoroughly cowed, retreated in panic. In the words of the historian Thomas Carlyle, the Convention was saved by "a whiff of grapeshot,"[22] but more accurately, the Revolution was saved by Napoleon's willingness to act decisively, even ruthlessly, in a crisis.

An eighteenth-century French cannoneer. Napoleon turned such cannons on the rioting mobs of peasants that stormed the National Convention in 1795. His ruthless though effective action made him an instant hero.

A Note on the Calendar

Napoleon's defense of the Convention took place on October 5, 1795, but in some histories the date is given as 13 Vendémiaire, III. This is because, in its efforts to wipe out the past, the Revolution adopted its own calendar, numbering years from the adoption of the constitution of 1792. In addition, the new calendar eliminated religious or mythological associations from the names of the days and months, giving them instead names that referred to some "natural" event. *Vendémiaire,* which lasted from September 22 to October 21 on the discarded Gregorian calendar and "month of vintage," corresponded to the period in which grapes were usually harvested. April 20 through May 19 became *Floréal,* "month of flowers"; July 19 through August 17 was *Thermidor,* "month of heat"; and so on. Each month was to have thirty days with five special days left over (six in leap years).

Eventually people grew tired of the confusion, not to mention the disadvantages, of working with a calendar different from that used by all the rest of the world. If, for example, a businessman ordered a shipment from Greece, could he expect it to arrive on January 23, 1798, or 4 Pluviose, VI? In 1802 France returned to the Gregorian calendar.

Too Near the Hero

Far more than actions at Toulon, Napoleon's defense of the Convention made him the hero of the moment. The new constitution was allowed to take effect. Ironically, under its terms, the real power lay not with the legislature but with a Directory of five men. Not surprisingly, Paul Barras was one of the five. Within a few days, Napoleon received his reward—perhaps the one he had bargained for with Barras. He was promoted to commander of the Army of the Interior. In less than three years, he had progressed from Corsican political refugee to the command of all soldiers stationed within the borders of France.

Only later did the members of the Directory realize how they had jeopardized

---

Love Aside . . .

In The Age of Napoleon, *Will and Ariel Durant quote Napoleon's memory of some advice from Paul Barras.*

"He assured me that she belonged to both the old and the new society, and that this fact would bring me more support; that her house was the best in Paris, and would rid me of my Corsican name; finally that through this marriage I should become quite French."

---

themselves. Here was an astonishingly able and frighteningly ambitious hero, one who might easily be a popular choice to take over the government. By placing him in charge of an army in their own backyard, they had handed him the means to bring about a coup d'état.

The situation was also unsatisfactory to Napoleon, however. He was still intent on advancing his military career. The activities of the Army of the Interior—guard duty and maintaining law and order—were unlikely to gain him either further promotion or glory. He craved battle.

A solution was at hand by the spring of 1796. The commander of French troops in Italy, found to be thoroughly incompetent, was to be replaced. Napoleon received the assignment, one that would prove to be the real beginning of his reputation as a military genius. On March 11, two days after his marriage to Josephine, he left for Italy.

Napoleon as commander of the French troops in Italy. This was the first portrait ever painted of Napoleon. It portrays him at the beginning of his military career.

4 To Italy and Egypt

At the end of the eighteenth century, Italy was not the single, unified country we know today. In effect, it was many countries. The Kingdom of the Two Sicilies comprised the toe and ankle of the Italian boot as well as the large island of Sicily itself. Central Italia contained the Papal States, a number of small jurisdictions governed by the pope in Rome. To the north as far as Switzerland was a hodgepodge of city-states, petty kingdoms, and dukedoms,

all carryovers from the glory days of the Renaissance: Venice, Genoa, and the others had been the artistic and trade capitals of Europe. But the Italian states had not wielded any real power in centuries. Since the mid-1500s, the various "countries" of the Italian peninsula had been under the control of other nations; Austria had held the reins for the past hundred years. The large northern territory of Milan was ruled directly from Vienna as part of the

When Napoleon arrived at his new command in Italy, his troops were demoralized, starving, and ill equipped. His personal charisma and strategic genius quickly turned them into a victorious fighting unit.

Austrian empire. Other states were ruled indirectly—they were allowed the appearance of independence only as long as their puppet kings and dukes followed the dictates of Austria.

In Paris, the Directory envisioned the Italian campaign as part of a grand, three-pronged strategy, with success in Italy the least important part. Napoleon's forces were expected to hold the Austrians at bay along the Franco-Italian border and perhaps make modest advances, while the main thrusts against the Germans to the north and east were launched by other French generals. Once the Germans had been conquered, the successful generals could turn south and join Napoleon in defeating the Austrians. It was a fine plan, but after initial success, the northern and eastern prongs came to naught.

The army Napoleon had been sent to command was disintegrating. Four years of defeat, disease, and desertion had whittled the original force of 106,000 men down to 63,000, but even that was only a "paper army." The actual number of effective soldiers who could be put into the field numbered a mere 37,600, about half the number of Austrian soldiers arrayed against them.

Morale had plummeted. The preceding commander had divided his army into small detachments spread along several hundred miles of the Italian border. This left them vulnerable to attack from the Austrians, from British warships sailing the Mediterranean, and even from local guerrillas. The soldiers had not been paid in months, supplies and equipment were nonexistent, and, after several years in the country, they had little to gain by foraging locally for food. Several battalions had no shoes. Few had enough muskets to go around. There was little cavalry or artillery. Such hardships were all the more galling because just over the Alps lay the fertile Italian plains of Lombardy. Moreover, moving from camp to camp were royalist agents, spreading mutinous sentiments.

Napoleon Takes Command

Even the most flattering portraits painted of Napoleon during his lifetime fail to reveal the fire and energy perceived by those who served him. Some of it was in his eyes, some in his voice. Many contemporaries described how his eyes burned almost hypnotically in an otherwise ordinary face and how his voice crackled with command. "From under his deep forehead there flashed, despite his sallow face, the eyes of genius, deep-seated, large and of a greyish-blue color, and before their glance and the words of authority that issued from his thin, pale lips, all bowed low."[23]

Napoleon took command of his army in late March 1796. If the common soldiers were growing rebellious, the same could be said for the staff officers he inherited. They were all at least ten years older than he and far more experienced. Each felt himself to be more deserving of command than this Corsican upstart. As they approached their first meeting with the new general, they sneered among themselves at his lack of height, his sallow complexion, and his barbarous accent. To a man, they were certain his appointment had come as a political deal rather than on merit (and to some extent they were right). "But at their first meeting with him they were awed into quick obedience by

The Truth of Military Genius

The great historian Arnold Toynbee in A Study of History *examined military genius since the beginning of recorded time. He believed it arose from a surprising source.*

"The military genius is the general who repeatedly succeeds in divining the unpredictable by guesswork or intuition; and most of the historic military geniuses—commanders of such diverse temperament and outlook as Cromwell and Napoleon—have recognized clearly that manpower and munition-power and intelligence and strategy are not the talismans that have brought them their victories. After estimating all measurable and manageable factors at their full value—insisting that 'God is on the side of the big battalions,' that 'God helps those who help themselves,' that you should 'trust in God and keep your powder dry'—they have admitted frankly that, when all is said and done, victory cannot be predicted by thought or commanded by will because it comes in the end from a source to which neither thought nor will has access. . . . the outcome of an encounter . . . arises, in the likeness of a new creation, out of the encounter itself."

Napoleon as First Consul of France.

Napoleon bests the enemy's general in hand-to-hand combat and forces his surrender. Napoleon's willingness to lead the battle charge gained him his men's respect and the nickname "the Little Corporal."

the confident clarity with which he explained his plans and gave his orders."[24]

It actually took a little more than two weeks before Napoleon was ready to go on the offensive. In the meantime, he raised the soldiers' morale considerably by somehow contriving to have them paid part of what they were owed. Perhaps even more buoying to their spirits was this proclama-

tion to the troops: the general promised them the plunder of Italy if they could win.

He faced a combined army of Austrians and Sardinians that outnumbered him two to one but was divided into three parts. If he could bring all his force to bear on any one of the three parts, he would have numerical superiority at the point of attack. The soldiers of the puppet kingdom of Sardinia, guarding the westernmost border, were the weak link, if only because they were ill disposed to fight to the death for their Austrian masters. Napoleon secretly moved his army into position and on April 11 began a series of attacks that within two weeks forced the Sardinian army to retreat to the city of Turin and take itself out of the war.

> In those battles the young commander impressed his subordinates with his keen and quick perception of developments, needs, and opportunities, his clear and decisive orders, the logic and success of tactics completing the foresight of strategy that often caught the enemy on flank or rear. The older generals learned to obey him with confidence in his vision and judgment; the younger officers . . . developed for him a devotion that repeatedly faced death in his cause. When, after these victories, the exhausted survivors reached the heights of Mount Zemoto—from which they could view the sunlit plains of Lombardy—many of them broke out in a spontaneous salute to the youth who had led them so brilliantly.[25]

Amid his triumphs, Napoleon himself was suffering. He was, in a word, lovesick. After all, he had been married but two days before beginning this expedition.

He sent an officer to Paris to bring Josephine to him, but the man returned with the news that she was ill and could not come at this time. The officer reported that she might possibly be pregnant. Napoleon's spirits soared. He hoped for a son. But the report was wrong.

Meanwhile, there was the Austrian army to deal with. In May he confronted the main force at Lodi. The Austrians had retired to the far side of a river and could be attacked only by crossing a 200-meter wooden bridge under withering fire. Napoleon dispatched his cavalry with orders to follow the river until they found a place to ford, then attack from the flank. When the French cavalry appeared, the Austrians were taken temporarily by surprise, and the French infantry started across the bridge. Heavy fire drove them back. Napoleon rushed forward and led the charge himself. The Austrians were routed. The French soldiers were thrilled by their commander's willingness to expose himself to fire. They began calling him "the Little Corporal," for corporals, not generals, normally led men into the hottest battle spots.

At about the same time, Napoleon received orders from the Directory that he

recognized as sheer folly. He was ordered to divide his army in two and turn half of it over to another general, who would pursue the Austrians; he was to use his half to attack the Papal States. Napoleon expected a strong counterattack from Austria, making a division of his army suicidal. Furthermore, the Italians had been treating the French as their liberators from the Austrian yoke, an attitude he encouraged. But he also knew that a physical attack on the Papal States would turn staunchly Roman Catholic Italy against him. He decided to risk his career by refusing the order. Instead, he offered to resign and turn his entire army over to a general of the Directory's choice. Faced with explaining to the people how they could lose the only general who was winning battles, the politicians of the Directory quickly backed down.

In August 1796, an overwhelming Austrian force, outnumbering Napoleon's army three to one, advanced on the French. They were led by Count Dagobart Sigismund von Wurmser, an officer who had been one of the victors against the northern French attacks. Napoleon was ready. He surprised von Wurmser with an attack at Castiglione and took 15,000 Austrian prisoners. Then, with-

Napoleon leads his troops to take a strategically important bridge at the Battle of Arcole during his first Italian campaign against the Austrians. His army routed the Austrians again and again until all of northern Italy was under French—and Napoleon's—control.

out allowing his opponent to regroup, Napoleon pursued him and defeated him twice more. Von Wurmser's army retreated to the city of Mantua, where Napoleon placed it under siege.

No sooner was von Wurmser neutralized than a second Austrian army of 60,000 appeared. Leaving a small contingent to continue the siege at Mantua, Napoleon moved against this new force. In a three-day battle at Arcole, where once more the general himself led his troops across a crucial bridge, the Austrians were sent reeling. Again, Napoleon followed quickly. At Rivoli, the Austrians lost 30,000 men. The remnants of their once mighty army retreated to Austria. When von Wurmser learned of the

defeat, he recognized his position at Mantua was hopeless and surrendered. All of northern Italy was under Napoleon.

Napoleon Takes Italy

Napoleon entered Italy as a liberator. "Peoples of Italy!" he proclaimed, "The French army comes to break your chains. The French nation is the friend of all nations; receive us with trust! Your property, your religion, your customs will be respected. We shall wage war like generous enemies, for our only quarrel is with the tyrants who have enslaved you."[26]

Leonardo da Vinci's Mona Lisa today hangs not in an Italian museum but in France's Louvre because Napoleon took it and many other Italian art treasures to France as spoils of war.

The Italians soon found out exactly what it meant to be liberated by Napoleon. "Napoleon incorporated Milan and other cities into a Republic of Lombardy, whose citizens were to share with the French in liberty, equality, fraternity, and taxes."[27] He could explain, quite logically, that the liberated must contribute to their liberation. The rich were to be heavily taxed, and the towns were persuaded (or ordered) to contribute to the upkeep of the French troops.

This was not an entirely bad deal, for by wining, dining, and otherwise placating the French soldiers, the towns for the most part avoided the horrors of looting and pillage. As a matter of fact, Napoleon had a few looters shot (though most got off with a warning). Regardless, the soldiers quickly learned that there was no need for brutality when the rewards of victory were being handed to them freely.

The major benefactors of Napoleon's occupation were the French people, right down to the present day. The vast art treasures of Italy—paintings, statues, jewelry—were boxed up and shipped to Paris to stock the Louvre and other museums. One of the paintings sent north was the Mona Lisa by Leonardo da Vinci, perhaps the world's most famous work of art. The art confiscated was estimated as worth tens of millions of dollars in 1800; today the value would run to nine or ten digits.

All this was done under the auspices of a six-man delegation sent from Paris under the innocent-sounding name of the Government Commission for the Research of Artistic and Scientific Objects in Conquered Countries. Some historians have insisted that Napoleon himself took no personal gain from all this. The fact remains that he went to Italy a poor man and returned rich. In Italy there was a saying, "Not all Frenchmen are robbers, but a good many are." In Italian, that's "Non tutti francesi sono ladroni, ma *buona parte.*"

Next, Napoleon turned to the Papal States. Pope Pius VI, the predecessor of the man who would agree to preside over the coronation of Napoleon eight years later, was "asked" to turn over the states of Bologna, Ferrara, Ravenna, and Ancona to the French for relieving the papacy of its Austrian oppressors (and, although it went unmentioned, to keep Napoleon from marching into the Vatican). What is called "extortion" between individuals becomes "diplomacy" between nations. On February 19, 1797, Pius VI not only surrendered the requested states but paid a 15,000 franc indemnity to help cover the French army's expenses in bringing freedom to Italy.

Austria was still a threat. Napoleon didn't wait for another counterattack. He advanced to within 60 miles of the capital, Vienna. In October, Austria sued for peace. Although he could not legally negotiate for the French government, Napoleon did so anyway, dictating the terms of the Treaty of Campo Formio, by which Austria left the war after ceding to France both Belgium and Lombardy, which was already lost. As a sop, Napoleon handed the supposedly free city-state of Venice to Austria.

Return to Paris

While Napoleon was becoming a French national hero in Italy, the French government was on shaky ground in Paris. The

---

For the Troops

In this excerpt from the Durants' Age of Napoleon, *Napoleon rouses his men to invade Italy by sympathy.*

"Soldiers, you are hungry and naked. The Republic owes you much, but she has not the means to pay her debts. I am come to lead you into the most fertile plains that the sun beholds. Rich provinces, opulent towns; all shall be at your disposal. Soldiers! with such a prospect before you, can you fail in courage and constancy?"

Directory was never popular. By 1797, its inefficiency had brought the idea of a monarchy back in favor among many French people. The current government was unable to solve food shortages, reduce unemployment, or curb inflation. Despite Napoleon's victories, many believed the war was being handled incompetently in Paris. People began to remember Louis XVI as not such a bad king after all, and to long for the old ways. When a conservative majority on the Directory seemed likely to turn away from the Revolution and perhaps even reinstate a monarchy, Paul Barras and his republican cohorts had the answer—another coup d'état. Word was sent to Napoleon in Italy, urging him to return and lend his military genius to the proposed coup, but he was too canny to let himself be used. He sent one of his officers. In early September, the conservatives were unseated. This coup, unlike previous ones, was bloodless; the vanquished conservatives escaped the guillotine and were instead exiled to French Guiana in South America. Although the republicans maintained a tenuous hold on power, they could not stop the populace from yearning for a strong leader who would make everything right.

On December 5, Napoleon returned to Paris as the greatest hero in France. He was feted by republicans, conservatives, and all shades between. For his part, the Man of the Moment spoke, dressed, and behaved modestly, betraying no signs of vaulting ambition. He seemed to avoid the public eye—while appearing just often enough at carefully selected sites and ceremonies to remind all that he was on the scene. Certainly, as long as he remained in Paris, Paul Barras and the Directory felt at risk. Thus they conceived a plan for

Napoleon offers one of his soldiers some tobacco. Napoleon's friendship with his men, unusual for a general, earned him their loyalty and devotion.

Napoleon to lead an invasion of England. The general knew that England had not been successfully invaded since 1066 and understood that as long as the British navy was the most powerful in the world, the island was not likely to succumb again. Instead of England, he chose Egypt.

On to Egypt

Egypt had a recorded history that went back nearly 5,000 years. The pyramids of Egypt had been in place for more than 4,000 years. Its leaders, the pharaohs, were once the kings of kings. But, by the time it came under Napoleon's gaze, Egypt was controlled by the Mameluk Turks as part of the Ottoman Empire, which included most of the land rimming the eastern Mediterranean. The Ottoman Empire was allied with England against the French. To strike at Egypt was a blow against Turkey, of course; but more important, it was a blow against France's most dangerous enemy, England. From Egypt France could disrupt British trade with the Middle East and even threaten India, the most valuable part of the British Empire. Strategically, a foray into Egypt made sense. At the same time, Napoleon was a student of history; he knew that those two ancient world conquerors,

Alexander the Great and Julius Caesar, had captured Egypt. Now it was his turn.

The expedition was enormous. One hundred thirty transports were protected by thirteen ships of the line, seven frigates, and eighty-five smaller warships. The army consisted of 38,000 fully equipped troops, including many veterans of the Italian campaign. In addition, there were 16,000 support people, and a number of scientists, historians, and scholars brought along to study the mysterious ancient civilization of Egypt. Josephine wanted to come too, but Napoleon refused that. He did, however, take along her son Eugene. This armada set sail from Toulon on May 19, 1798.

Napoleon before the Great Sphinx of Egypt. Napoleon's conquest of Egypt was a strategic victory for France, but to Napoleon himself it was a personal victory. It placed him among the ranks of Alexander the Great and Julius Caesar, two other world conquerors for whom Egypt was a prized conquest.

Ironically, the greatest victor in the Egyptian campaign was scholarship. The learned men accompanying the invasion studied everything they could find and eventually produced a massive twenty-four volume study of Egypt and its history. However, the most important discovery was made by a man known to us only as Bouchard. In a town near Alexandria, he found a flat stone containing inscriptions in Greek, Demotic Egyptian (a simplified form of the Egyptian language), and hieroglyphics, the strange, up-to-then undecipherable, "picture writing" of the ancient Egyptians. Eventually, it was realized that each language section of what came to be called the Rosetta Stone proclaimed the same message, and, because scholars could read Greek, they were finally able to decipher hieroglyphics and learn the long, complex history of the Egyptians from ancient accounts.

"The time which I passed in Egypt was the most delightful of my life," Napoleon wrote later. "In Egypt I found myself free from the wearisome restraints of civilization. I dreamed all sorts of things, and I saw how all that I dreamed might be realized."[28] Be that as it may, the Egyptian campaign was a military disaster.

A contemporary painting depicts Napoleon leading a charge against the Turks in Egypt. Although Napoleon easily conquered Egypt, he could not hold it. The British destroyed the French ships at Alexandria, trapping the French army.

The Rosetta Stone was found by the French scholars who accompanied Napoleon to Egypt. With it, scientists could finally decipher Egyptian hieroglyphs and unlock the mysteries of ancient Egypt.

Having landed in Egypt, Napoleon's army had little trouble winning the land. Not a single battle or skirmish was lost while Napoleon led his troops. But England still ruled the waves. At the end of July, Admiral Horatio Nelson, England's greatest naval leader, caught the French fleet at Alexandria before it could slip back across the Mediterranean. The two sides were evenly matched in guns and ships, but there was no contest in fighting skill. All but two of the large French warships were captured or destroyed. The French admiral was killed, along with 1,750 men, and another 1,500 were wounded. The British lost 218 men with 672 more wounded.

Although victorious, Napoleon's army was now cut off from home, unable to be reinforced or resupplied, and unable to retreat. With a hostile population all around them—the Mameluk sultan had called for a holy war against the invaders—the French had become prisoners of the land they'd conquered. Eventually, all would be lost.

Napoleon attempted to march out with 13,000 men by going east then north through Palestine and Syria (modern Israel and Lebanon). His small army won several notable victories, but eventually Turkish defenders and the blazing summer climate forced them to return exhausted to Cairo. There, several Turkish attacks were repulsed, but it was now only a matter of time before the Turks and British would combine to destroy the invaders. The dire predicament of the isolated army was unknown to the people at home. Napoleon well understood the value of propaganda. In France, they heard only of victory after victory in Egypt.

The other war news was not so good. The British had put together another coalition of powers, which had driven the French out of Germany and recaptured much of Italy. While Napoleon was bottled up in Egypt, all the gains he had made on the continent were disappearing. Eventually he received an order from the Directory, sent long before the loss of his fleet, to return to France. There was nothing that could be done in Egypt. He promised his soldiers that if he could change things in France, he would rescue them. Then, in one of the two frigates that remained, he set sail for France.

5 The First Consul

Napoleon returned to France an even greater hero than he'd been when he left. To his conquest of Italy had been added, apparently, the conquest of Egypt. The French people did not realize that the army he left behind was cut off from reinforcements and ultimately doomed. It would be two years before the soldiers he had led in triumph to the pyramids would be forced to surrender to the British. By then, only half of the original army would remain, the rest having been lost to illness and costly victories. Yet, despite its disastrous conclusion, to the extent that it had raised Napoleon's star even higher, the Egyptian expedition was a triumph.

It was a surprise then, after traveling to universal cheers from the Mediterranean coast to Paris, to be greeted coolly by the members of the Directory. The politicians even debated among themselves the possibility of bringing Napoleon to trial for deserting his post but quickly decided that such a move against the most popular man in France would only bring the wrath of the populace down on their own heads.

The reason for the Directory's lukewarm reception was that his arrival forced them to deal with a new and powerful factor in their plans for yet another coup d'état. Coups had become almost annual affairs with the Directory. One had pre-

ceded Napoleon's last visit to Paris and another had taken place while he was in Egypt. When he arrived this time, no fewer than three of the five members of the Directory were planning takeovers. Each director hoped to make Napoleon, with his ability, his popularity, and the loyalty of the army, a personal ally.

Napoleon's relationship with his wife Josephine was stormy, but she remained the love of his life. He claimed to love her more than the glories of war.

Taking Control

Before stepping onto the larger stage provided by French politics, Napoleon had a domestic problem to settle. Months earlier, he'd received word that Josephine had been unfaithful to him. Although he had been less than a loyal husband himself while in Egypt, he returned home determined to confront and divorce her. But she was not in Paris when he arrived. In a development worthy of comic opera, Josephine had learned of his intentions and set out to meet him along his path to Paris only to miss him when he took an unexpected route. In Paris, Napoleon received her ancient former father-in-law, the marquis de Beauharnais, who begged, "Whatever her faults, forget them; do not cast dishonor upon my white head, and upon a family that holds you in honor."[29] Napoleon's brothers, Joseph and Lucien, however, urged him to throw her out. Canny Paul Barras took the practical side and cautioned that a scandal would hurt the general's political career.

When Josephine returned to the Bonaparte residence, her husband was in an upstairs bedroom with the door locked against her. She sat sobbing on the stairs. Her children, Hortense and Eugene, made entreaties. At last, he opened the door to them. He later wrote, "I was profoundly stirred. I could not bear the sobs of those two children. I asked myself, should they be made the victims of their mother's failing? I reached out, caught hold of Eugene's arm and drew him back to me. Then Hortense came . . . with her mother. . . . What was there to say? One cannot be human without being heir to human weaknesses."[30]

Napoleon's View of Human Nature

Although Napoleon was contemptuous of others' ideologies, he had one of his own, according to J. Christopher Herold in The Age of Napoleon.

"He did not search for final causes, since he tacitly assumed that the final cause was power; compared to the ideas [of the leading thinkers of the day], Napoleon's stand out in stark and lucid simplicity. The art of government is to keep the people reasonably happy by giving them what they want and to obtain from them all one can get. To do this one must know men. In Napoleon's view, men were neither good nor bad—they were what circumstances made them. The good could be corrupted; as for the bad, 'a legislator must know how to take advantage of even the defects of those he wants to govern.' 'Men are like ciphers: they acquire their value merely from their position.'"

Napoleon was almost always portrayed as self-assured and in control. In this painting he is the calm center amid the turmoil that occurred when he forced the Directory to resign in 1799.

With that settled, at least for the time being, the head of the Bonaparte home turned to becoming head of France.

He considered joining Paul Barras in yet another takeover, but Barras's talent lay in grasping power, not exercising it. Another Barras-led coup would produce only more of the same unsatisfactory government. Barras had twisted and turned his way through five years to remain the only one of the original directors still in office, but at last he'd run out of tricks. Other plotters, even royalists intent on restoring a Bourbon king, visited Napoleon. Finally, he decided to ally himself with Emmanuel Sieyès, a former priest turned politician, who wanted to estab-

lish a more compact, authoritarian government—thinking that fell in line with Napoleon's own. He told Sieyès, "We have no government because we have no constitution, or at least not the one we need; your genius must give us one."[31] Sieyès believed Napoleon would be his military backing; Napoleon had a different agenda.

Sieyès was useful to Napoleon in preparing his route to leadership. The supporters of Sieyès convinced the legislators that a crisis was imminent and that only a new, more centralized government under a new constitution could save the day. Although the Directory initiated laws, the legislature (made up of the Council of Ancients and the Council of Five Hundred) ultimately decided their constitutionality. Under Sieyès's orchestration, the legislature moved to the palace of St. Cloud in the Paris suburbs, where they would be less accessible to the mob. At the same time, the members of the Directory were pressured by Sieyès's allies into resigning in favor of a new government. Then Napoleon, the protector of the legislature in 1795, was sent for and again placed in charge of the troops guarding Paris. He accepted with a pledge that left him room to maneuver: "We want a republic based on liberty, equality, and the sacred principles of national representation. We will have it, I swear!"[32] During the events that followed, he could maintain that he was keeping that pledge. On November 11, 1799, Napoleon surrounded the palace at St. Cloud with 500 troops.

Some of the legislators were having second thoughts about the path they were following. Sieyès's plan called for replacing the five-headed Directory with a "Consulate" of three consuls. Under such a setup, one man would surely take control. And, by then, even Sieyès realized that the one would be General Bonaparte. Napoleon addressed the Council of Five Hundred, haranguing them to accept the consul idea, but for once he was unable to summon the right words. His speech was incoherent and merely added to the legislators' distrust. Cries of "Outlaw the dictator!" filled the hall. The general beat a hasty retreat.

Outside, among his loyal troops, he insisted that some of the legislators had tried to attack him with daggers. Napoleon's brother Lucien was president of the Council of Five Hundred and had been staunchly assisting Sieyès in ramming the

How to Lead

"Men are moved by two levers only: fear and self-interest," J. Christopher Herold *quotes the emperor in* The Age of Napoleon. *Herold continues, drawing on Napoleon's memoirs.*

"To make them behave, one must play on both levers. The ruler must teach them respect ('Nothing is more salutary than a terrible example given at the right time'), but the lesson must be given sparingly ('Great men are never cruel without necessity'). The ruler must also satisfy the people's basic wants. Liberty is not among these. Few men really care about it: 'Consequently it can be repressed with impunity. Liberty means a good civil code. The only thing modern nations care for is property.' The masses desire equality, but 'they would gladly renounce it if everyone could entertain the hope of rising to the top. . . . What must be done then is to give everybody the hope of being able to rise.'"

Lucien Bonaparte, Napoleon's younger brother, was president of the Council of Five Hundred, one of the houses of the French legislature. His dramatic speech to the council in 1799 helped put Napoleon at France's helm.

In Office

Technically, Napoleon was only one of three provisional consuls who would divide governmental powers among themselves until a new constitution could be drafted and adopted. In reality, he was the master of France. The question for historians has been whether Napoleon's ascendancy to dictatorship signaled the end of the Revolution, or, as he himself maintained, consolidated its gains. Was he the son of the Revolution or its assassin? There is plenty of ammunition for both sides.

In truth, the people of France no longer wanted democracy. After ten years, enthusiasm for the Revolution had waned. Continuous warfare, ever-higher taxes, prices, and unemployment, the Reign of Terror, a succession of coups d'état, and the selfish and woefully ineffective Directory had combined to discredit government by the people. France wished only for a government that would be honest, efficient, and stable. The people quickly embraced the Consulate because they believed Napoleon could answer their prayers.

No one expected—and only a few desired—that having once gained control, Napoleon would relinquish it. Within hours of assuming office, he began issuing directives and decrees. The other two provisional consuls were Sieyès, who busied himself with writing the constitution, and Roger Ducos, who proved to be no more than a rubber stamp to Napoleon's orders. When Sieyès presented his constitution, after Napoleon had made certain necessary corrections, the Consulate was firmly in the saddle and the three consuls had been designated first, second, and third. Not surpris-

Consulate down the throats of the assembly. He told the soldiers that the council was being terrorized by a few stiletto-armed representatives (no doubt paid by England), who stood in the way of the will of the majority. Then, in a dramatic gesture, he pointed a sword at Napoleon's heart and declared that should his brother ever attack liberty, he himself would strike the fatal blow.

Great theater and effective! Bayonets fixed, the soldiers marched into the hall and drove out the legislators. A few hours later, some of the lawmakers—those who could be counted upon to vote correctly—were readmitted. Thus on November 9, 1799, while soldiers stood by with their bayonets still at the ready, the assemblage solemnly decreed that the Directory would give way to the Consulate. It was all quite legal.

ingly, the First Consul, the only one that counted, was Napoleon Bonaparte.

Sieyès had been an early and avid supporter of the Revolution, but by 1799 he had lost most of his faith in the wisdom of the people. Napoleon, of course, never had any such faith to lose. "Men are like ciphers," he said. "They acquire their value merely from their position . . . [they] are moved by two levers only: fear and self-interest."[33] The new constitution reflected this cynical view by placing all power in the hands of the leaders. Two months after it was put into effect, the constitution was submitted to a popular vote. The polls

This marble bas-relief depicts Napoleon as First Consul of France. As First Consul, Napoleon supervised the formation of a new constitution and government.

NAPOLEON

stayed open for a month, during which time the government exerted all possible pressure to produce a favorable vote. The results 3,500,000 for and 1,500 against—were certainly overwhelming, but roughly half the eligible voters did not bother to vote.

Under the new constitution, all France was divided into districts called *départements;* these were further divided into *arrondissements;* and these divided once more into *cantons.* Every adult male could vote—but only for the *communal list,* which was made up of one-tenth of the adult males in a canton. Those elected could then vote for the *departmental list,* which consisted of one-tenth of the communal list. In turn, the victors in this contest could elect the *national list,* drawn from one-tenth of their members. Only those on the national list could hold high national office. So, although male suffrage was universal, only one in a thousand could aspire to a role of national leadership. Government was, in effect, a pyramid. But, instead of resting on a base, power under the new constitution flowed from the top.

But, even most of those at the top were severely limited. The *Council of State,* which could draft bills to be submitted to the legislature, consisted of forty members chosen from the national list by the First Consul. In other words, only the First Consul—Napoleon—or his underlings could initiate laws. The legislature was divided into three parts: the *Senate,* chosen by the Second and Third Consuls from the national list, could decide on the constitutionality of laws; the *Tribunate,* chosen by the Senate, could discuss proposed bills but not vote on them; and the *Legislative Body,* also chosen by the Senate, could vote on bills but not discuss them. The structure had the appearance of a democratic republic, but in reality every member of the national government was directly or indirectly answerable to the First Consul.

To give Napoleon his due, during the first year of the new constitution, he listened politely to the discussions of the Tribunate and occasionally allowed their wishes to override his own. It was only in the second year of the Consulate that he saw to it that the legislature was packed with supporters he could depend on to vote as he wished.

The entire country was reorganized as Napoleon's personal responsibility. He appointed a Minister of the Interior, which

Napoleon, as First Consul, swears in the first Council of State, forty men chosen by him to draft bills to be submitted to the legislature.

The symbol of equality, one of the ideals of the French Revolution. Under Napoleon's rule, however, equality, like liberty, was an illusion.

in turn appointed a prefect to supervise each *département* and appointed the mayors of the communities within that district. In effect, Napoleon controlled the government from top to bottom.

The old cries of liberty, equality, fraternity were heard no more. Napoleon believed that the people did not really want liberty, "consequently it can be repressed with impunity. . . . Liberty means a good civil code. The only thing modern nations care about is property."[34] In other words, a state that is efficiently run, with laws that are clear and not unusually oppressive, needn't bother itself with such trappings as the Rights of Man. To protect this new order, Napoleon instituted government censorship of the press and the most effective secret police in Europe.

Napoleon and the Revolution

Historian Robin W. Winks in Western Civilization: A Brief History *is one who identifies Napoleon as the culmination of the French Revolution.*

"Under [Napoleon's] reign, the bones of the Revolution—uniform law codes, reorganized public finance, the stabilization of the official orders of government and society, and the protection of property and power—took on their permanent flesh. Out of the myriad complaints, plans, alternatives, and secondary and tertiary revolutions of the period 1778–1804, the government of Napoleon strengthened and established those that appealed most strongly to the groups which supported him and whose complaints had effectively launched the Revolution—the middle classes, with their stability, wealth, and demands for opportunities open to talent, energy, and work."

Equality was another buzzword that could be ignored. Men talked about equality, but what they really wanted was the chance to rise above their neighbors. "What must be done," Napoleon counseled, "is to give everybody the hope of being able to rise."[35] Under his dictatorship, the ability to advance one's station in life was severely limited, but the *illusion* that one could rise to the heights was carefully maintained. Was not Napoleon himself the supreme example?

Winning the People

The first problem for a dictator is to obtain power; the second is to secure it. In 1802 Napoleon became First Consul for Life by way of yet another overwhelmingly favorable popular vote. As much as modernists may abhor a dictatorship, the fact remains that Napoleon had the majority of the people behind him.

There were good reasons for his popularity. One of his first moves was to rescind a Directory-installed tax of 20 to 30 percent on all incomes above a moderate level. He allowed banished supporters of the Revolution to return to France, among them Lafayette, a hero of the American Revolution. He revoked another unpopular Directory law that allowed prominent citizens throughout France to be held hostage until their districts paid for any crimes committed against the government. He enacted several laws to help businessmen, and he helped heal old wounds by canceling several hate-feeding festivals decreed during the revolution, such as a celebration of the beheading of Louis XVI.

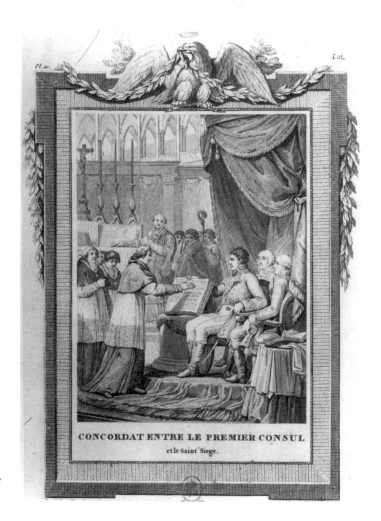

An engraving representing the Concordat of 1801, in which Napoleon restored the spiritual authority of the Roman Catholic Church in France.

Of the many reforms Napoleon's supporters could point to, four stand out and are important even today. He inaugurated a complete system of national education that included primary schools, secondary schools, technical training schools, and colleges. The University of France was established to supervise all schools and curricula, as well as the licensing of teachers. Napoleon's purpose was to produce good and loyal citizens. The government chose the schoolbooks and dictated what ideas teachers could teach. Students were expected to memorize such thoughts as "Christians owe to the prince who governs them, and we owe in particular to Napoleon . . . love, respect, obedience, [loyalty], military service." [36]

His fiscal reforms brought a balanced budget and rigid economy to government. His tax system was fair, especially in comparison to what people had endured under the Directory. In 1800 he established the Bank of France.

By an agreement called the Concordat of 1801, he ended the break that the Revolution had brought with the Roman Catholic Church. Napoleon himself was certainly not religious, but he recognized the power of religion among the people and believed he could use it for his own purposes by appearing as a friend of the Church. The spiritual leadership of the Church was recognized, and Roman Catholicism was declared to be the majority religion of France. Nonetheless, religious freedom was guaranteed to Protestants and other minority religions. The Church gave up the claims it had maintained to the Papal States lost to France during the Revolution. The government continued to appoint members of the clergy and to pay their salaries, but the pope gained the right to confirm or refuse appointments to the clergy.

The greatest of the domestic reforms by far was the *Code Napoléon,* a new civil code for France. Prior to this, laws in France were a crazy quilt. In the south, Roman law dating back more than 1,500 years was the base. In the north, customary, or common, law applied, some left over from as long ago as ancient Gaul. Moreover, there were 366 separate local law codes scattered around the country. A particular act might be legal in one place and illegal elsewhere, with punishments ranging from a light fine in one municipality to a long prison term in another. Travelers

The University of France was founded as part of Napoleon's effort to establish a system of national education.

were constantly at risk. Intercommunity squabbles were impossible to resolve.

The job of unsnarling this hodge-podge so that one code of law might apply throughout France was enormous. Twice the leaders of the Revolution had tried to do it, and twice they had failed. It took Napoleon's boundless energy to bring it to pass. He named a commission, the Commission of Legislation, to study all existing laws and propose ways of bringing them together. When the commission lagged, he prodded it. When it was at loggerheads, he broke the stalemate. Of the 102 sessions in which the commission met, he presided over 57. Often he intervened in the discussions to make important suggestions.

Some criticized the Code because it contradicted many of the goals of the Revolution. For example, in disputes between employers and employees, the Code gave employers preference over employees; in any disagreement between them, the employer was to be believed. Fathers were given despotic rights over the family; they could even imprison their children. Illegitimate children were barred from inheritance. Divorce was made much harder to obtain. And women's rights all but disappeared. "Women should stick to knitting," Napoleon said. "The husband must possess the absolute power and right to say to his wife: 'Madam, you shall not go out, you shall not go to the theater, you shall not receive such and such a person; for the children you will bear shall be mine.'"[37]

Many of the most important achievements of the Revolution were retained, however, such as religious freedom and the laws that allowed poor farmers to purchase the land they worked on. In all, the Code represented a compromise of old and new. On balance, it incorporated more of the Revolution than of the ancien régime.

It took until 1810 to complete the work. The resulting document, though harsh in some of its penalties, meant that at last people in all parts of the land and from all stations in life were treated equally under the law. The Code Napoléon is still the basis of French law, and, carried beyond the borders by French armies, it became the foundation of civil law in Belgium, Holland, Italy, many South American countries, and the state of Louisiana.

At the end of his life, Napoleon said, "My glory is not to have won forty battles, for Waterloo's defeat will destroy the memory of as many victories. But what nothing will destroy, what will live eternally is my Civil Code."[38] Most historians agree.

Even Napoleon's critics marveled at his executive ability. France had perhaps never been so efficiently governed. Detractors were more likely to find fault with his methods than with his results. In truth, one obvious weakness was that he literally had his hand in everything. Authority was never completely delegated to others. What then would happen at some future date, when a lesser mortal controlled the apparatus this Napoleon had put in place?

6 The Emperor Strikes

When Napoleon became First Consul, France had been almost constantly at war for a decade.

Always there was England. From the earliest days of the French Revolution, England had been France's most determined and most dangerous foe. The two adversaries faced each other across the narrow English Channel—on a clear day, England's coast can be seen from the shore of France—each dedicated to the downfall of the other. Invasion from France was a constant worry in England, but fear of physical domination was not the primary source of British antagonism. England was ahead of France and the rest of the world in embracing the Industrial Revolution. By the end of the eighteenth century, it had become the greatest manufacturer in the world. But the presence of any dominant power on the continent of Europe was a threat to that position because it would put control of the major export markets for British goods into other hands. Without its thriving export business, England would wither economically. Only France could dominate Europe. Spain was in eclipse. Portugal, Belgium, the Netherlands, and the Scandinavian countries were too small. Germany, like Italy, was fragmented into many small states. Neither Russia nor Austria was industrially advanced enough to be a threat.

Therefore, England's purpose in fighting France was not to crush it but to maintain a balance of power on the continent and to keep all markets open to British goods.

The British strategy was always the same: control the seas with its navy while forming a coalition of European nations to do most of the land fighting against France. Historians sometimes differentiate among the various conflicts of this period by using such names as War of the Second Coalition or War of the Fourth Coalition. In truth, however, there was an almost continuous war, matching France against England, from 1792 until Napoleon's abdication. Other countries, such as Austria, Portugal, Russia, Prussia (the strongest German state), Spain, Sweden, and Turkey sometimes participated in the various coalitions put together by England, but some of these countries were at times allied with France. We needn't attempt here to sort out the comings and goings of allies. Suffice it to state that England and France never allied with each other.

Defeat and Victory

Napoleon needed a spate of peace to consolidate his gains. But only victory could bring peace. In May 1800, he donned his

Napoleon's victory over Austria at the Battle of Marengo in northwest Italy was one of his most celebrated. His victories against the Austrians in Italy and Germany weakened France's rival, England, and brought a short-lived peace to Europe.

general's uniform once more. In one of his most celebrated campaigns, he led his troops across the Alps and once more crushed the Austrians, this time at the Battle of Marengo in June. A few months later in Germany, he defeated them again at Hohenlinden. Austria was forced to sue for peace again, ending the land war in Europe. Shorn of its allies, England continued the sea war for a few more months, but there was no victory in sight. The government that had led the war against France was swept out of office and replaced by one more conciliatory. By the Treaty of Amiens in March 1802, peace came to Europe.

It lasted but a scant fifteen months. During that time, Napoleon continued to reorganize his nation. One of his actions that is sometimes criticized was the sale to the United States, for a mere $15 million, of the Louisiana Territory—a huge expanse of land between the Mississippi River and the Rocky Mountains.

To many Americans, the Louisiana Purchase of 1803 seems a decidedly short-sighted act on the part of Napoleon. The purchase nearly doubled U.S. territory and made western expansion possible. It is without doubt one of the most important events in this nation's history. However, from Napoleon's standpoint it was not a bad deal at all. He had become convinced that France stood no chance of retaining the territory. The old enemy England controlled the sea and could destroy any army he chose to send to Louisiana. A small army had already been lost on the Caribbean island of Hispaniola. If he simply sat tight, the Louisiana Territory would be taken from him by either England or the United States. If the former, his enemy would be immeasurably strengthened; if the latter, a nation would arise that might one day rival England. In giving up Louisiana, he lost something he did not really possess, filled his treasury, and, at least potentially, weakened England. It was simply good business. Reportedly, when he shook hands on the deal with the American ambassador, he whispered, "You shall fight England again."

Among Napoleon's reforms in France was the replacement of the old system of weights and measures with the metric system, an improvement that is still in place. He also at this time created the Legion of Honor, a decoration for outstanding civic or military service.

Sooner or later he would cross swords with England again. To that end, he began making preparations for the next war while in the midst of peace. The English were particularly disturbed when he embarked on a large shipbuilding program, especially when they saw that many of the new vessels were flat-bottomed barges, ideal for ferrying troops across the channel.

The fate of his domain when he was no longer there to tend it also concerned Napoleon. The necessity, as he saw it, was to make his succession hereditary. The only way to do this was to become emperor.

Napoleon's warlike preparations, certain economic policies designed to hurt England, and the prospect of his becoming emperor were too much for the British. Before he could even take his throne, Napoleon was once more at war with his old enemy. Soon after his coronation, England formed still another coalition, this one including Austria, Russia, and Prussia.

The one sure way to put an end to England's opposition was to invade the island and conquer it. Napoleon felt certain that could he but put his large and well-trained army on English soil, he could easily dispose of this enemy. The trick was

Napoleon's decision to sell the Louisiana Territory to the United States in 1803 was an important event in U.S. history, allowing continued western expansion.

Napoleon and the Revolution, #2

Edward McNall Burns in Western Civilizations *argues that far from continuing the ideas of the Revolution, Napoleon represented a reaction against those ideas.*

"The period of Napoleon's rule . . . may properly be regarded as the initial stage of the nineteenth-century reaction against the liberal ideas which had made the Revolution possible. To be sure, Napoleon professed to be in sympathy with some of these ideals, but he established a form of government scarcely compatible with any of them. His real aim, so far as it concerned the work of the Revolution, was to preserve those achievements which comported with national greatness and with his own ambitions for military glory. In other words, he fostered and strengthened Revolutionary patriotism and continued those accomplishments of his predecessors which could be adapted to the purposes of concentrated government. But liberty in the sense of the inviolability of personal rights meant nothing to him; in fact, he declared that what the French people needed was not liberty but equality. Moreover, he interpreted equality as meaning little more than a fair opportunity for all regardless of birth. That is, he did not propose to restore serfdom or to give back the land to the old nobility, but neither did he plan any restrictions upon the economic activities of the rich."

Napoleon the emperor.

British admiral Horatio Nelson (center, left) died in the Battle of Trafalgar in 1805, but not before destroying the French navy and Napoleon's hopes of invading England.

getting there. Although he referred to the English Channel as "a mere ditch," he estimated that in any crossing, 20,000 of his 120,000 troops would drown. "One loses that many in battle every time," he rationalized.[39] That was not the whole of it, however. If the British navy were free to attack his transports, French losses would be staggering. Somehow, the British ships must be kept out of the channel, if only temporarily. "Let us be masters of the straits for six hours," Napoleon said, "and we shall be masters of the world."[40]

Any dreams Napoleon may have held of invading England were ended on Octo-

ber 21, 1805, by the sea battle of Trafalgar, one of the pivotal naval engagements of all time. Under the command of Admiral Pierre de Villeneuve, the French had put together a large force. The British fleet under Admiral Horatio Nelson chased them across the Atlantic to the West Indies and back to Europe again. For a brief time, the English Channel was unprotected, but other events kept Napoleon from taking advantage. Villeneuve put in at the Spanish port of Cádiz (Spain being at that time allied to France), where he nearly doubled his fleet by adding 14 Spanish warships. Napoleon ordered Villeneuve to attack the British. Villeneuve held numerical superiority over Nelson, 33 ships to 27. They met near Trafalgar, a low, sandy cape on the southern Spanish coast at the western entrance to the Strait of Gibraltar.

Nelson completely outsailed his opponent, surprising him by cutting through the French battle line. Warships in the early nineteenth century had few guns that could fire forward or backward, so when the British cut through the train of French ships, they were able to blast those to either side while the French were helpless to return fire. More than half of Villeneuve's ships were captured or destroyed; the British did not lose a ship. The French admiral committed suicide. Nelson, considered England's greatest admiral, was fatally wounded by a sniper in the fighting, but he had reinforced England's control of the seas and ended any threat of invasion by Napoleon. Trafalgar Square in London, named for the victory, is dominated by a large statue of Nelson.

With all hope of invading England gone, Napoleon was forced to fall back on a strategy of defeating the land armies of

Having routed their armies with superior strategy, Napoleon persuades the Russian and Austrian generals to surrender at the Battle of Austerlitz in eastern Europe. Napoleon fought the battle on December 2, 1805, the first anniversary of his coronation as emperor of France.

the coalition again and again until England once more stood alone. He outmaneuvered the Austrian army at Ulm and marched into Vienna with ease. Then he turned north, where a huge Russian army was en route to combine with a large Austrian force. Napoleon had 70,000 men; his foes had 85,000. He carefully chose the ground for the battle, the low hills near Austerlitz, a small village in what later became Czechoslovakia. On the eve of battle, he strode among his soldiers. According to one veteran, he seemed to know each man by name.

The Battle of Austerlitz took place on December 2, 1805—the first anniversary of Napoleon's coronation. It is sometimes called the Battle of the Three Emperors, because the Russians were under the command of Czar Alexander I and the Austrians under Francis I; the French, of course, were led by Napoleon I.

Napoleon had carefully concealed the bulk of his troops behind some high ground in the center of his position. His right flank appeared weak, and the enemy began a mass attack there just as he had anticipated. At his signal, the concealed men burst from their hiding place and moved swiftly to encircle the Russians and Austrians. When they realized they were under attack from all sides, the allied troops tried to flee across a frozen lake, but Napoleon's artillery pounded them, breaking up the ice, and sending many to a watery death. By four o'clock in the afternoon, it was all over. The allied losses of 27,000 were three times those of the French. The next day, Napoleon told his army, "I will lead you back to France. There . . . my people will welcome you with joy, and you will only have to say 'I was at the battle of Austerlitz' for people to exclaim, 'Behold a hero!'"[41]

Austerlitz has been called Napoleon's masterpiece. Perhaps in no other victory did his strategy succeed with such clockwork precision. Coming as it did less than two months after Trafalgar, it restored Napoleon's mystique as master of the continent. Austria was knocked out of the war and forced to sign a humiliating peace treaty. Russia was forced to retreat to its own borders.

Reportedly, William Pitt, the aged British prime minister who had tirelessly put together one coalition after another to oppose Napoleon, was on his deathbed when he received word of Austerlitz. Spying a

Napoleon named his brother Jerome king of Westphalia in 1807. Installing his many siblings as rulers of Europe helped reinforce Napoleon's power.

map of Europe across the room, he ordered, "Roll up that map. It will not be wanted these ten years." In effect, he was saying that all Europe was now France. That was an exaggeration, but only a slight one. The Prussian army was destroyed at the battles of Jena and Auerstadt in October 1806. The following June, at the Battle of Friedland, it was Russia's turn. By the end of 1807, no army in Europe was capable of standing against France. Napoleon then proceeded to redraw boundaries at his will.

At the height of the emperor's power in 1810–1811, the so-called Empire of the French included modern-day Belgium, the Netherlands, Corsica, the Papal States, and the Balkans from the Danube River down to Montenegro. France directly controlled Spain, Switzerland, the kingdoms of Italy and Naples (the remainder of Italy not included in the Papal States), a combination of 300 small German states Napoleon called the Confederation of the Rhine, and what is today Poland. Austria, Prussia, Denmark, and Norway were allied with France, much as lambs ally with a wolf. Portugal, Sweden, and Russia were presumably not part of the empire, but certainly in no position to dispute it.

One of Napoleon's ways of ensuring a friendly government among the satellite nations was to place his relatives on their thrones. Joseph ruled the kingdom of Naples for two years and then was appointed king of Spain in 1808. Louis became king of Holland (the Netherlands) in 1806. Jerome was made king of Westphalia (carved out of the German states) in 1807. One sister, Caroline, was married to the man Napoleon chose to succeed Joseph as king of Naples. Another sister, Elisa, became grand duchess of Tuscany,

The Other Brothers Bonaparte

David Stacton in The Bonapartes *briefly profiles Napoleon's brothers.*

"Jerome was an extravagant incompetent. Louis was a contumacious invalid. Joseph was of a saving disposition and of a prudence unsuited to military life. Lucien's contribution to the family amity was an excessive uxoriousness and a complacent sense of self-congratulated virtue. He produced fourteen children by two wives and was devoted to all of them. He was also jealous and envious of the Emperor, to whom he liked to give advice and toward whom he felt superior, both in accomplishment and intellect."

one of the Italian states. And Josephine's son Eugene was named viceroy of the kingdom of Italy. All of them were known by the surname Napoleon.

Yet, Napoleon's empire could not rest secure as long as England remained uncowed just across the channel.

The Continental System

If the English refused to fight him on land and the emperor dared not oppose them at sea, what was left? Napoleon settled on economic warfare. He called his plan the *Continental System,* but basically it was a blockade. European ports were closed to England. He reasoned that an England unable to export its goods would be forced to pay for its imports with gold, noting with satisfaction that as an island nation, England imported heavily. The more English gold used for this purpose, the less would be available for the English government to

expend in stirring up and subsidizing allies in anti-French coalitions. Furthermore, French economists told Napoleon that when English exports dried up, the nation's economy would crash, spreading unemployment and misery. The opposing government would be swept out of office and replaced by one more receptive to French considerations. Perhaps an English Revolution would result.

France, of course, would be hurt by the lack of imports, but France did not rely as completely on trade as did the British. A few businessmen would be bankrupted, a few banks would fail. What was that compared to the damage inflicted on England?

But merely closing French ports to the British was only part of the game. To be effective, all Europe must be locked against England. It took a small army of customs inspectors to monitor all the ports under French control—and a large army of soldiers to protect the inspectors, enforce their decrees, and guard against smuggling. When Russia sued for peace in 1807, it was given generous terms in return for agreeing to seal its ports to England. At that point, Napoleon had no doubt that the Continental System would systematically bring the British to their knees.

It was not to be. The English were hurt badly but not nearly to the extent that Napoleon had hoped. Dearly missed were iron from Sweden and lumber from Russia. Inflation rose, as did unemployment. Revolution was perhaps talked about in alehouses, but it never came to pass. Cut off from Europe, the British were able to survive on trade with their ever-expanding empire all over the world. That, and through the stubborn efforts of smugglers.

Meanwhile, France suffered with the loss of certain imports, which had become necessities as far as the French people were concerned. Sugar and coffee were particularly missed. Napoleon encouraged the finding of substitutes. Chicory replaced coffee and is drunk by many today. Attempts were made to create sugar from grapes and even turnips. Eventually, it was discovered that sugar beets could be grown in France, and the large sugar beet industry that survives today resulted. But substitutes could not be found for many materials and manufactured goods. Smuggling was rampant. The Continental System sprung leaks all along the French coast. Along less friendly shorelines, the leaks became gushers.

A Mistake

The most obvious gap in the Continental System was Portugal, England's longtime ally. Goods flowed from England to Portugal unabated, and from Portugal into all of Europe. In 1807 Napoleon sent troops to occupy the little country. The Portuguese royal family fled to Brazil.

In disciplining Portugal, however, Napoleon came to realize that Spain, a supposed ally, was paying only lip service to the Continental System while continuing to trade as before. The ease with which he had overrun Portugal led Napoleon to assume he could do the same with Spain. He forced the royal family to abdicate and called in Joseph from Naples to take the throne. Meanwhile, his army defeated the Spanish army every time they met.

But the situation was not settled. The Spanish people, among the staunchest Roman Catholics in Europe, were shocked to have their Church-blessed royalty summarily replaced by someone who spoke

Napoleon's brother Joseph was sent by the emperor to rule Spain after Napoleon forced the Spanish royal family to give up the throne. The result was open rebellion in Spain.

Spanish master Francisco Goya painted this scene of a mass execution of Spanish rebels by Napoleon's forces. The Catholic artist symbolizes the unjust suffering of his people in the central figure, who, white-clad and bathed in light, his arms outstretched like the crucified Christ, submits to death.

barely a word of their language. Joseph tried to be a good king to his new subjects, but word quickly spread that the foreign king was an atheist, and whatever the truth of the allegation, most Spaniards believed it. All over Spain, the people rose in revolt. Napoleon was faced with a guerrilla war. All his battlefield brilliance was for naught against a determined enemy that struck small but telling blows from ambush by night, then became simple, peaceful farmers by day. How do you array artillery against the wind? How can you march against an army that is everywhere? The French resorted to atrocities such as mass executions, but these outrages only increased the hatred the Spanish held for them.

The great Spanish artist Francisco Goya produced a number of paintings and etchings detailing the horrors of the war. One of his most famous works shows a faceless, seemingly inhuman, French firing squad aligned against a group of helpless peasants standing amid bodies of those already slain. Some of the peasants pray, cry, or cover their faces, but the central figure, clad in white, continues to stare out at his executioners.

To aid the guerrillas, the British landed a small army of 14,000 men in Portugal. Ably led by the duke of Wellington, this force began staging lightning thrusts into Spain, overwhelming small contingents, and then withdrawing to safety. To counter the guerrillas and the British "commando raids," Napoleon was forced to send more and more troops into Spain. Ultimately, he had 250,000 soldiers mired in an unwinnable war on the Iberian peninsula.

These were troops he could ill afford to lose, for while France was bleeding to death in Spain, old enemies were gathering for another thrust from the east.

7 Decline

One of the supreme ironies of Napoleon's career had to do with the two-edged sword of nationalism—that devotion to one's native land or to one's ethnic group that can

A soldier in Napoleon's Imperial Guard stands proudly erect. Napoleon was able to inspire nationalistic fervor in his troops and to promote himself as an icon of France.

lead people to move mountains or to destroy them. French nationalism was his "secret weapon" as he rose to power. But the nationalistic feelings that he instilled in other countries helped to bring him down.

Before the French Revolution, nationalism was not a strong current in much of Europe. People were more likely to follow a king or a duke than their country's call. After all, large areas of land, along with the people who lived there, were routinely handed from one side to another when a new peace was signed. Regions were renamed and life went on. It was difficult to think of oneself as a German in any unique sense when one might wake on the morrow to find oneself a subject of France. Usually, the only difference was in the identity of the tax collector.

The French Revolution, however, with its strident cries of "equality" changed that in France. If all the French were equal, then assuredly there must be some quality or qualities that set them apart from the non-French. And, whatever those traits might be, they were embodied in the French nation—France. The soldiers who opposed foreign enemies during the early days of the Revolution were not fighting so much to preserve the new revolutionary government as they were to preserve France (which happened to be in the midst of a revolution). Considering how quickly government heads could be changed by the fall of the guillotine's blade, soldiers could hardly be expected to fight for whoever happened to be in charge in Paris at that moment; but they could and did fight bravely to save the nation—the idea—of France. The enemies of France were quick to recognize that its soldiers fought with a dedication and spirit seldom found among their own troops. Napoleon is supposed to have said, "Every French soldier carries a marshal's baton in his knapsack." He meant that the equality of the French made them better leaders, and he underlined that conviction with battlefield promotions. This was the fervor of nationalism.

Napoleon expanded and deepened such loyalties, shamelessly exhorting his "soldiers of France" to go forward and conquer for the greater glory of the motherland. Later, he became in his own eyes and the eyes of most of his subjects the living embodiment of the nation. "I am the state," he declared.

Each new country conquered was assured that it was being "liberated" from its oppressive rulers. Only later did the people learn that they were also being liberated from their treasures for the greater good of France. But in the meantime, they had been addressed as Italians or Spaniards or Germans. Napoleon even redrew the map of Europe to make much of divided Italy into one nation and then did the same with more than 300 small German states. He created an independent Poland as a buffer against Russia. While Napoleon did these things primarily to make conquered regions easier to govern, his actions had the unexpected result of causing the people within those regions to begin thinking

Adolf Hitler and the Nazi party rose to power on the heady rhetoric of German nationalism. Nazism brought nationalism, born in Napoleon's France, to a deadly extreme.

of themselves as nations. Soon, they found themselves united in at least one idea—to throw out the French. It was this bare beginning of nationalism that enabled the Spanish to continue their guerrilla war against the invaders in the face of terrible retributions. Thus, nationalistic ideas that had aided Napoleon in his rise were turned against him.

Nationalism set loose by the French Revolution and nurtured by Napoleon became one of the strongest forces on this planet during the nineteenth and twentieth centuries. It has made possible the creation of the nations of the world. It has also led to innumerable wars and terrible atrocities. Once one begins to think of oneself as belonging to a special group, it becomes evident that great things may be accomplished for the betterment of that group. But, at the same time, those outside

that special elect become lesser beings—
sometimes no longer even quite human.
And when that attitude develops, a holo-
caust may ensue.

Divorce

At the end of the first decade of the nineteenth century, Napoleon's empire appeared secure. The civil war in Spain was a
distraction, but the guerrillas could not ultimately win. England still opposed him on
the sea, but he held Europe. The Austrians
once more took the field against his army
in 1809 and were again soundly defeated.

France was the most powerful nation on
earth—and Napoleon's personal monu-
ment.

But the emperor was entering his for-
ties. Who might succeed him to the
throne? What would become of Napoleonic France once Napoleon was no
more? As a student of history, Napoleon
knew that great empires had been destroyed by squabbles for power among various factions when the strong leader fell.
History had shown that such divisions
could be avoided if the succession to the
throne were hereditary. Loyalties were easily transferred from father to son: "The
king is dead; long live the king!" But the
emperor had no son. Napoleon worried

Napoleon's marriage to Austrian princess Marie Louise. Though he still loved Josephine, he
needed an heir, which she could not provide. The marriage also inserted Napoleon's heirs
into the royal line of the Austrian Hapsburgs, powerful rulers of the Holy Roman Empire.

The young empress Marie Louise fulfilled her intended role by giving birth to a son, Napoleon II, within one year of her marriage to the French emperor.

that his sudden death or even a serious illness could bring down the empire he had so painstakingly built with passion, energy, and blood. He must have a son and heir.

Sadly, he told Josephine he must divorce her. She fainted and could not be revived for several minutes. "I shall always love you," he explained, "but politics has no heart; it has only a head."[42] He could forgive all her faults except her failure—and, of course, he was certain it was HER failure—to give him a son. She would be well provided for and would want for nothing (except, of course, a husband). On December 16, 1809, they were divorced by the Senate. A few weeks later, the archbishop of Paris pronounced the marriage annulled. In Catholic France, most disapproved of the separation. Nor were they pleased with his choice for the next empress.

Marie Louise was an Austrian princess, eighteen years old, healthy though plain, and reasonably intelligent. She had been taught for much of her life that the most evil man on earth was Napoleon Bonaparte. She also knew that a princess was a political card to be played in high-stakes power struggles between nations. Her duty was to submit. The marriage of its princess to the French emperor gained Austria, so often Napoleon's opponent, a bargaining chip with Europe's master. For his part, Napoleon gained a means of providing him with a son, and, by marrying royalty, he confirmed his own royal estate. On March 12, 1810, Marie Louise was married to Napoleon by proxy; he was represented by one of his officers. Then a parade of 83 carriages wound its ceremonial way for two weeks to Paris. There followed another civil marriage ceremony and a religious one. Most of the cardinals of Paris refused to attend because the pope had not annulled the emperor's marriage to Josephine. Napoleon had them banished to the far provinces of France.

Marie Louise was never as popular with the French as Josephine had been, but she had no outstanding faults. Eventually, the people came to regard her as a symbol of France's triumph over foreign foes. Her acceptance was greatly enhanced when, on March 20, 1811, she gave birth to Napoleon II. The baby was immediately proclaimed the king of Rome. Reportedly, Marie Louise was so afraid she might hurt the child that she refused to hold him.

Napoleon delighted in his son and appeared to like his young wife, but he visited Josephine often—so often that Marie Louise began to pout. Thereafter, he limited his trips but continued to write countless letters to Josephine, each beginning "My Love."

The Tide Turns

Napoleon always believed that a general had about ten years at the top of his profession, after which he would begin to lose some of his strategic abilities. Critics have pointed out that he apparently fell victim to this diminution of talent himself. In his first decade of generalship, his victories were based on quick maneuvers and strategy. But, after 1807, he tended to rely more on massed attacks, with their corresponding high number of casualties. This, critics suggest, indicates that his generalship was slipping.

Defenders cite two reasons for this apparent change in strategy. First, constant fighting over a long period had cost most of the trained troops with which Napoleon had won his early victories. The more raw recruits he was forced to thrust into the line as replacements for seasoned veterans, the more his strategy had to be simplified. Additionally, many of the replacements were from conquered allies, making for communication problems in issuing orders.

A second reason for simplified strategy was that battles were being fought with progressively bigger armies. In 1796 Napoleon led 35,000 men into Italy. Twelve years

The aging general Napoleon at the head of his troops. After a decade of brilliant military conquests, Napoleon's leadership abilities seemed to diminish. He relied more on numeric superiority than on exceptional strategies to win his battles.

Napoleon the Propagandist

By mid-1811, the war in Spain was as good as lost. Although he certainly knew that, on June 16 Napoleon gave the following confident speech, quoted by Michael Glover in The Peninsular War, *to the legislature.*

"Since 1809 most of the fortified towns in Spain have been taken by memorable sieges; the rebels have repeatedly been beaten in battle. England understands that the war is coming into its final phase. She has found that her position has changed. Money and intrigue will no longer keep the war going. From being no more than an auxiliary, she has had to take a leading role. All her regular troops are in the Peninsula. England, Scotland and Ireland are stripped of troops. Rivers of English blood have flowed in battles which have proved glorious for the French army. Our struggle against Carthage, which they thought could be decided on the seas or beyond them, will now be settled on the plains of Spain. A clap of thunder will put an end to the Spanish business. It will finish the English army. It will avenge Europe and Asia by ending this second Punic war."

later, French casualties at the Battle of Wagram—a victory—totaled almost that many! Huge armies could simply not maneuver with the same speed as smaller forces.

If Napoleon was suffering "burnout," his work schedule was clearly part of the problem. As master of Europe, he was concerned with all diplomatic dealings with friend and foe. As emperor, he dictated orders on every aspect of life in his realm, from the education of girls in public schools to government encouragement of the growing of sugar beets. And, as commander in chief, he personally led his army on the eastern front while keeping one eye on what has happening in Spain. Twenty-hour workdays were his norm.

For all his strength and abilities, Napoleon had also been lucky. For a decade and a half, he'd thrived under a favorable star. But in 1811, that star began to dim.

The civil war in Spain continued to drag on, using more and more men and materials. "My Spanish ulcer," Napoleon called it.[43] Had he been able to lead the army in Spain himself, he might have been able to end the conflict, but the combination of Spanish guerrillas and the duke of Wellington's small English-Portuguese force proved too much for the generals Napoleon sent in his stead.

The real enemy, he knew, was England, safe behind its wall of fighting ships. Since he could not attack England with his army, he could only use the Continental System

Lord Wellington's English-Portuguese force proved too much for Napoleon's generals.

bar English goods. Actually, a goodly amount of English products had continued all along to be brought into Russia under various false papers, but now the floodgates were open. Napoleon wrote to Czar Alexander I: "Your Majesty no longer has any friendship for me; in the eyes of England and Europe our alliance no longer exists."[44] When Alexander made no reply, Napoleon began readying for another war.

Alexander had been upset by Napoleon's marriage to Marie Louise. He saw a Franco-Austrian alliance as a threat to Russia. Believing war to be inevitable, he mobilized 240,000 men but held scant hope that his army could defeat Napoleon

Czar Alexander I of Russia perceived Napoleon's marriage to Austria's Marie Louise as a Franco-Austrian alliance that threatened Russia. He therefore readied his troops for war.

to turn the screws more tightly on its economy. Then, in 1811, a serious depression struck France. Rightly or wrongly, people blamed the Continental System. Napoleon was forced to issue licenses allowing the import of certain British goods into France.

That exception enraged Russia. Under the Treaty of Tilsit signed in 1807, vanquished Russia had been given very lenient treatment in exchange for its agreeing to honor the Continental System, but the end of trade with England worked a real hardship on Russia's economy. Then, after several years of belt tightening, Russia suddenly saw France relax restrictions on itself while expecting others to continue to

Napoleon's troops enter Moscow, September 15, 1812. The French found the city almost deserted. They looted the city, most of which was later burned to the ground. His offer of a truce refused, Napoleon retreated from the city in mid-October, but his army was devastated by the murderous Russian winter.

on any battlefield. This time, however, there would be one major change. Always before, in Napoleon's victories over Russia, the czar's armies had been attacking. This time they would be withdrawing into the huge expanse of Russia. "We have vast spaces in which to retreat," Alexander said. "We shall leave it to our climate, to our winter, to wage our war."[45]

The Russian Campaign

Napoleon pulled out all the stops and raised a huge army—650,000 men—for the invasion of Russia. The *Grande Armée* was the largest force he had ever had at his disposal, but only a part of it was French. Much of it was made up of soldiers from Poland, Switzerland, Holland, Italy, Germany, and Austria—the nations France had defeated. Few of these troops were happy to be fighting for France; some were near rebellion.

The French strategy was simple: march into Russia, overwhelm the czar's army, and destroy it, forcing Alexander to sue for a humiliating peace. On June 24, 1812, Napoleon crossed the Neman River and began the drive into Russia. But the Russians refused to cooperate. Instead of meeting him in open battle, they embarked on a seemingly endless retreat. By August, the

French were deeper into Russia than Napoleon ever expected to go, spread out along a 700-mile line, and still they had not been able to engage the enemy in a major battle.

Napoleon took a chance. With a force of 150,000, he advanced on Moscow, the Russian capital. Finally, at Borodino, about 70 miles from Moscow, the Russian army stood its ground. The result was a victory of sorts for the French as they drove the Russians back. But the cost was heavy for Napoleon's men, and the czar's army was able to withdraw while it was still an effective fighting force.

A week later, on September 15, Napoleon entered Moscow only to find the city largely deserted. He moved into the Kremlin, marveling at the beauty of the near-empty city: "Under every point of view, it might bear comparison with any of the capitals of Europe; the greater number of them it surpassed."[46] Looters were soon at work, seeking any treasures Muscovites had left behind. That night, the city began to burn. Most buildings were of wood construction. Despite the best efforts of French firefighters, the city blazed for five days until two-thirds of it was ashes. Napoleon had 400 suspected Russian arsonists shot, although the fire may have been started by looting French troops. Either way, it left Napoleon in a terribly exposed position with the dreaded Russian winter approaching.

He sent word to Alexander offering a truce and decrying the burning of the city: "Such a deed is as useless as it is atrocious."[47] He blamed the city's governor for ordering the destruction. The Russian czar did not reply. He told one of his officers that rather than sign a shameful peace treaty with Napoleon, he would "let my beard grow to my breast, and . . . go and eat potatoes in Siberia."[48] And while Napoleon waited, the season grew later. On October 8, he ordered a retreat.

Napoleon's retreat from Moscow was a disaster. The Russians still steadfastly avoided a major fight, preferring to snipe at and harass the retreating French. Any straggler separated from the 60-mile column

Napoleon the Propagandist, #2

According to Robert B. Holtman in The Napoleonic Revolution, *Napoleon was frustrated by public opinion.*

"The population of Paris is a collection of blockheads who believe the most absurd reports. . . . I respect the decisions of public opinion when they are justly formed; but it has its caprices which we ought to learn to despise. *It is the task of the government, and of those who support it, to enlighten the public, not to follow it in its meanderings.*" [italics added]

The Road Builder

In The Napoleonic Revolution, *Robert B. Holtman points out an often-overlooked accomplishment.*

"The most important long-range contribution the Napoleonic period made to commerce was the improvement of transportation. Even though Napoleon built or improved roads for purposes more military than economic, they did facilitate commerce. Particularly was this true of the roads built in the Alps. During his fifteen years in power, Napoleon built or repaired 40,000 miles of roads. Not all of them were imperial routes; many were farm-to-market roads. At the end of his reign there were 33,000 kilometers of royal roads; 30,000 kilometers were open, but, in part as a result of the Allied invasion of France, only 12,000 were in good condition. Napoleon also built bridges, including four over the Seine at Paris and one over the Rhine at Kiel."

was as good as dead. Bands of Cossacks, skilled horsemen from Russia's southern frontier plains, staged deadly "hit-and-run" raids. In the meantime, the French were retreating through the very lands they had ravaged on their way in. They could find no food, and their summer-issue clothes were in tatters as the snow began to fall and the icy winds blew. The temperature dropped to 30 degrees below zero. Pack animals were slaughtered for food. The spoils of looters were discarded in snow drifts. Men froze in their tracks, or fell over as Russian snipers found their marks. "All along our way," reported one survivor, "we were forced to step over the dead or dying."[49]

Napoleon often marched beside his men in a vain effort to lift their spirits.

"Both officers and soldiers think only of protecting themselves from the terrible cold," wrote one of Napoleon's generals. "The road is littered with men frozen to death. The soldiers throw away their guns because they cannot hold them."[50] November turned into December, and still the French were trapped inside the country they had conquered.

The bridges over the Berezina River were the goal. Once the French crossed them, they would be in the comparative safety of Poland. But the Russians knew this too. Both sides raced for the river. The Russians arrived first and burned the bridges. Perhaps any general other than Napoleon would have surrendered there and then, but the Little Corporal wasn't ready to quit. He threw up a brilliant rear-

Napoleon's retreating army falls prey to the brutal Russian winter. Of 650,000 soldiers, only about 40,000 survived.

guard action, giving his men time to force pontoon bridges across the river.

A small part of his huge invading force escaped—40,000 soldiers—and only about half of them were ever able to fight again. Some 20,000 Prussian troops changed sides, but most of the Grand Army lay dead or captured. Napoleon desperately began raising another army for the attack he knew must come. Like vultures circling a dying animal, yet another British-led coalition, the fourth, began to prepare for the campaign of 1813.

Chapter

8 Fall

The armies of Europe gathered to crush Napoleon and France. Russia and Prussia joined together to wage a "war of liberation" in Germany. Francis I of Austria, though nominally still an ally of France and doubly tied through Napoleon's marriage to Marie Louise, seemed certain to join the coalition against his son-in-law. England was unable to throw its full weight into the coalition, having become involved across the sea in the War of 1812. (Napoleon's prediction that America would fight England again had come true.) But, despite this distraction, the British navy continued to blockade French ports.

Napoleon was not ready to concede. He had a few allies left. He could raise another army. Troops had to be withdrawn from Spain, virtually assuring the Spaniards and the duke of Wellington success in that arena, but the main threats were now in the east. Napoleon's strategy was to defeat the Russian-Prussian invaders quickly in Germany; that might convince Austria to stay out of the war. Beginning in March 1813, he won a series of battles that forced the Russian-Prussian combine to retreat. In June they signed an armistice.

With peace temporarily restored, the allies went about rebuilding their armies. In Sweden, the crown prince convinced the king to oppose Napoleon, adding an-

Jean-Victor Moreau, one of Napoleon's generals, had been exiled to America for plotting against the emperor. He returned in 1813 to advise the leaders of the nations allied against Napoleon. While at the side of Czar Alexander, he was slain by a French sniper at the Battle of Dresden.

other 25,000 men to the allied cause. Ironically, the crown prince of Sweden, Jean-Baptiste Jules Bernadotte, was a Frenchman who only a few years earlier had been one of Napoleon's most successful generals. In 1810, with their aging king childless, the Swedish legislature had asked Napoleon to supply one of his foremost generals as heir apparent. Now, as the future king of Sweden, Bernadotte wanted to position his new country on the winning side. Another of Napoleon's former generals, Jean-Victor Moreau, had been exiled to America for taking part in a plot on the emperor's life. He returned to offer his insights into Napoleonic strategy to the allies. Moreau's basic rule: attack Napoleon's army when Napoleon himself is elsewhere.

For two months, various peace proposals were exchanged without result. On August 9, Napoleon received a communiqué from Vienna, where the allies were gathered, that the truce would end the next day if he did not agree to their latest terms. He sent back a conditional acceptance, but it arrived in Vienna—perhaps as the allies wished and expected—too late. The truce had ended. On August 11, 1813, Austria officially came in on the side of the allies and the war began again.

On to Elba

Napoleon found himself facing three armies in a rough semicircle. From the north came Bernadotte and the Swedes; from the east, the Prussians; and from the southeast, the Austrians and the Russians. To meet this triple threat, he was forced to divide his own army into three parts. This had two disadvantages. First, he could not use his favorite strategy of concentrating his force to smash one opponent at a time. If, for example, he massed his troops to attack the Austrians, the way to Paris would be left open to the other two invading armies. A second disadvantage, perhaps the major one, was that Napoleon could personally command only one army at a time.

The emperor moved first against the Prussians in the middle, but was forced to break off there to repel the Austrian-Russian army moving up from the south. He met them at Dresden in the German state of Saxony. After two days of heavy fighting, the Austrians and Russians retreated, having lost 6,000 men. One of them was Moreau, the former French general. He died with Czar Alexander beside him. His last words: "I, Moreau, struck by a French shot, and dying amid the enemies of France."[51]

Dresden was a costly victory for Napoleon. Both sides had suffered heavy losses, but his could not be easily replaced. His opponents had a nearly bottomless reservoir of manpower, but, after twenty years of war, France was beginning to run on empty. In early October, Napoleon lost one more ally as Bavaria, another German state, jumped to the coalition.

On October 16, in the key battle of this European campaign, 160,000 soldiers under Napoleon faced 320,000 coalition troops at Leipzig in southeast Germany. The Battle of Leipzig is often called the Battle of Nations because so many countries were involved, but an accurate translation of the phrase (which was originally in German) is the *Slaughter* of Nations. Napoleon led his army brilliantly in bloody fighting on the first day. Had it ended there, he would have been declared the winner. But the day had cost him too many soldiers once again, and his artillery ammunition was nearly exhausted.

The emperor was exhausted, too—and ill. Years of battle, of twenty-hour workdays, of eating and sleeping in the saddle, had finally begun to take their toll. On the second day of battle, he was uncharacteristically hesitant. His proper action was to withdraw, regroup, and rearm, but instead he waited, sending peace feelers to the allied leaders. These were ignored, and still Napoleon waited. At last, it was too late. On the third day of battle, the allies attacked. Saxony, under the urging of Bernadotte, switched sides at a crucial moment, and what was left of the French army was crushed.

The war was lost, but Napoleon fought on with a brilliant series of delaying actions. His hope was to so frustrate the allies that they would at last offer an easy peace. But he had come out of Leipzig with only 60,000 troops, and with each new skirmish, no matter who won, that number was reduced. At the same time, like a giant machine that had been overworked and underfueled for too long, Napoleon's empire was flying apart. In Italy, Eugene retreated before forces that outnumbered his two to one. In Holland, the people rose

The Catalyst of Nationalism

Blending his own thoughts with those of others, Robert B. Holtman in The Napoleonic Revolution *explains Napoleon's influence on German nationalism.*

"In Germany Napoleon's drastic reduction in the number of states, started with the *Reichsdeputationshauptschluss* and continued with the organization of the Confederation of the Rhine, unwittingly promoted a feeling of nationalism. The French author François René Chateaubriand stated the matter well: 'Napoleon thought that by effacing so many frontiers and drawing all these strategic roads he was merely tracing the way from his barracks; in fact he was opening the road to a fatherland.' In destroying the Holy Roman Empire he cleared away a thousand-year-old obstacle to the development of nationality and a national spirit. As the American historian James Harvey Robinson wrote: 'Napoleon, in a somewhat incidental and left-handed fashion, did so much to promote the progress both of democratic institutions and of nationality in Western Europe that he may, in a sense, be regarded as the putative father of them both. . . . He is the founder of modern Germany.'"

Leaders of the allies discuss their strategy in the Battle of Leipzig in 1813. They eventually crushed the exhausted French army.

against their French conquerors. From lost Spain, Wellington crossed the border to invade France from the southwest. Within the country itself, a great economic depression brought widespread bankruptcies (blamed on the emperor). Many who had cheered Napoleon's every deed for more than a decade now cursed his name. The allies added to the unrest in December with the Declaration of Frankfurt, in which they announced that their enemy was not the French but Napoleon: "The Allied Powers are not making war on France. The Sovereigns [allied rulers] desire France to be great, strong, and happy."[52] Criticism of Napoleon that would have been considered treason only a short time before had become common.

Historians Will and Ariel Durant:

> Not much was needed to separate the people from the Emperor. The Senate and the Legislature were in open revolt against him, demanding a constitution with guarantees of freedom. On December 21 the Allies crossed the Rhine [River] into France. On December 29 the Senate sent Napoleon its assurances of loyalty and support. But on the same day Laine, member from royalist Bordeaux, read to the Legislature a report criticizing the "mistakes" and

Napoleon's energy, decisiveness, and military and political savvy brought himself and his country to primacy in Europe. His legacy has lasted to the present day.

Napoleon, exiled for life to the island of Elba, bids farewell to his son and his wife, Marie Louise. His family was not allowed to accompany him into exile. But exile simply allowed Napoleon to rest and make a dramatic comeback.

"excesses" of the imperial administration, praising "the happy sway of the Bourbons," and congratulating the Allies on "wishing to keep us within the limits of our own territory, and to repress an ambitious activity which for the last twenty years has been so fatal to all the peoples of Europe." The Legislature voted, 223 to 31, to have Laine's report printed. That evening Napoleon ordered the session closed."[53]

A delegation from the Legislature was sent to him on January 1 to wish him happy new year and, oh, by the way, about that constitution. . . . Napoleon exploded: "You are not the representatives of the nation . . . I alone am the representative of the people. After all, what is the throne? The throne is a man, and that man is my-self. It is I who can save France, and not you! . . . You shall have peace in three months, or I shall perish."[54]

But three months of fighting brought only further allied advances. Even the emperor was having second thoughts. He told a few trusted senators: "I do not fear to acknowledge that I have made war too long. I had conceived vast projects; I wished to secure to France the empire of the world. I was mistaken."[55]

On March 31, Napoleon raced to Paris to lead resistance. He arrived in the evening only to learn that the allies had entered the city that morning. Paris had not been fortified, and he was unwilling to see it destroyed by fighting. He turned away. Two days later, the Senate deposed him as emperor. Finally, on April 11, 1814, he gave up and abdicated his throne. The allied terms were surprisingly mild: he was exiled for life to Elba, an 86-square-mile island off the coast of Italy. He was to be regarded as the island's sovereign and even to receive a pension of 2 million francs a year from France. Neither his son nor Marie Louise was allowed to accompany him. Before leaving, he wrote to his first wife: "Never forget him who has never forgotten you and will never forget you."[56] A month later Josephine died.

The Bourbons returned to rule France. Louis XVI's son, Louis XVII, had died, so the allies installed a younger brother of the former king as Louis XVIII. The new king was nearly sixty, slow, and genial. He had spent time in England studying the British parliamentary system and was willing to serve as a constitutional (rather than an absolute) monarch. He also retained many of Napoleon's reforms, including the Code Napoleon, while relaxing restrictions on freedom of speech.

In September, the victorious allies met in Vienna for the important work of slicing up the Napoleonic empire among themselves. European politics was rapidly returning to normal.

The Hundred Days

Anyone who really believed that Napoleon Bonaparte would quietly live out his days, content to rule a pinpoint in the Mediterranean, didn't know the man. After a lifetime of ranging from one corner of Europe to another, of bending nations to his will, of changing the world with a snap of his fingers, he found Elba a living death. A short vacation from command restored his boundless energy. He began to plan a final roll of the dice.

In Paris, despite his best efforts, Louis XVIII was losing the popularity that had

Napoleon, alone on Elba, plans the battles he hopes will regain his and France's former power and glory.

On March 1, Napoleon landed on the French coast near Cannes with 1,100 men and began a march on Paris. His route was carefully chosen to pass through areas still loyal to him. At Grenoble, the commander of the Fifth Division of the army sent 500 soldiers to stop him. He strode forward. "Soldiers of the Fifth, I am your Emperor. Do you recognize me?" he shouted. He held his coat open. "If there is among you a soldier who would like to kill his Emperor, here I am."[57] The soldiers lowered their weapons and cheered him. *"Vive L'Empereur!"*

At every mile, his "army" grew. General Michel Ney, who had fought so many battles for Napoleon, was called before Louis XVIII and ordered to stop the march on

England's Duke of Wellington (below) joyfully greets Prussian general Gebhard von Blücher as Blücher's army comes to his aid against Napoleon at Waterloo.

Napoleon rallies the people of Grenoble to his cause as he makes his way from Elba to Paris, gathering an ever larger army along the way. Soldiers sent by the king to stop him ended up joining him instead.

greeted him on ascending the throne. Veterans who had fought for Napoleon loathed this Bourbon. The economy creaked along. The Church demanded restoration of all lands lost during the Revolution, which would have meant appropriating such lands from hundreds of thousands who had bought them. Old Jacobins decried the loss of many ideals of the Revolution. Many French people simply missed the excitement Napoleon had brought to their daily lives. And in Vienna, the allies continued to squabble for scraps as 1814 ended and 1815 began.

Paris. Ney promised to bring the Corsican back "in a cage," but when they met, old loyalties took over and Ney fell in beside his former commander.

Louis was forced to leave Paris. On March 20, amid great cheers, Napoleon arrived in the city and took over the government. He had regained the throne without firing a shot. At last, the allies in Vienna woke up. Once more they would have to defeat Napoleon in battle. They began readying another overpowering army to invade France in July. In the meantime, 200,000 troops in the Netherlands, under the commands of the duke of Wellington

and the Prussian general Gebhard von Blücher, were assigned to hold Napoleon at bay.

The emperor had no choice but to attack Wellington and Blücher. He dared not leave his flank exposed when the big invasion came which he expected in July. He managed to raise 120,000 men, many of them veterans of his earlier triumphs, and marched into the Netherlands. He planned to destroy Blücher's army first then wheel on Wellington, but Blücher disengaged from the battle and retreated in good order. Napoleon thought the Prussian was out of the fight, but in reality

The famous final defeat of Napoleon by Wellington's army at Waterloo. Deserted by his Imperial Guard, the emperor returned to Paris and again formally gave up his throne.

Blücher was circling around to come to the aid of Wellington. On June 18, Napoleon attacked the duke's army, but an overnight rain prevented him from getting his artillery into the battle until nearly noon. A longer bombardment might have helped. In the face of repeated charges, the duke's army of Redcoats stood firm along a low ridge near the small Belgian town of Waterloo. Learning that Blücher was approaching, Napoleon hurled one last charge, the elite Imperial Guard, ever victorious through eleven years. Wellington's men laid down a withering fire. Halfway up the hill, the Guard wavered and stopped. Then they turned and ran. Just then Blücher arrived to turn the French retreat into a rout.

All was lost. Napoleon returned to Paris and wrote out his final abdication. He named his son, then with Marie Louise in Austria, as his successor, but that was ignored. The boy never reigned; a sickly child, he died of tuberculosis at age twenty-one. General Ney was captured, and for his crime of joining his old commander, he was shot.

For several weeks after abdicating, Napoleon was a fugitive in France, protected by friends and admirers. He pondered what to do. Briefly he considered escaping to America, where he said he would study botany. On July 15, he surrendered himself to the captain of the British warship *Bellerophon* and was taken to England, where the government deliberated on what to do with him. Many were for execution, but that was a dangerous course. He would be thought a martyr by all those still loyal to him, and yet another war might result. Better to exile him again. But this time to a place from which he could never return. They settled on St. Helena, a

Napoleon II, though named as his father's successor, died at age twenty-one without ever ruling France.

volcanic island off the west coast of Africa, 700 miles from the nearest land. In this desolate wasteland, half the size of Elba, the man who had ruled the greatest empire since Rome lived out his final days. On May 5, 1821, he died.

Napoleon's death was attributed to natural causes, although four doctors disagreed on the exact malady, citing liver disease, stomach ulcers, and cancer. Not surprisingly, legends persist that he had been poisoned, perhaps by his British captors. In 1955 a Swedish poison expert noted that the symptoms Napoleon reportedly exhibited just before his death matched those of arsenic poisoning. Knowing that traces of arsenic remain in the hair of victims, the Swede succeeded

Napoleon, aged and in ill health, dictates his memoirs while in exile on the island of St. Helena. His words reveal his belief that he was only history's pawn.

"I have conceived many plans, but I was never free to execute one of them," he wrote. "For all that I held the rudder, and with a strong hand, the waves were a good deal stronger. I was never in truth my own master; I was always governed by circumstances."[58] Through it all, according to his version, every step he took, every battle, every law, every edict—*all of it*—was undertaken only for the greater glory and advancement of France. And, given but a little more time and luck, he would have brought peace, prosperity, and freedom to all of Europe. Perhaps when he said it, he believed it.

Napoleon's tomb in Paris. His body was brought to France from St. Helena in 1840. The passing years had also restored his former reputation as a national hero.

in obtaining snippets of Napoleon's hair cut from his head in his final days as keepsakes by loyal admirers. When the samples were tested, arsenic was discovered in apparently increasing amounts as Napoleon neared death. Although this finding lent credence to the poison theory, it should be noted that arsenic is found naturally in the soil of St. Helena. Arsenic can be and often has been fatally ingested by accident. Even suicide cannot entirely be ruled out. The endless boredom of St. Helena could have led him to decide on such a finish. For six years on that rocky island, the supreme man of action had nothing to do but watch the sun and dictate his memoirs.

Though historically valuable, these papers are largely self-serving. At times he explained himself as the pawn of history:

The Death of Napoleon

In Panati's Extraordinary Endings of Practically Everything and Everybody, *Charles Panati comments about the emperor's last days.*

"There is no question that Napoleon's doctors hastened his death. Beginning in the spring of 1821, Napoleon was in agonizing stomach and liver pain. His vomiting—combined with acute diarrhea from amoebic dysentery picked up on the island—severely dehydrated him. His physician at the time, Francisco Antommarchi, sent by the former emperor's relatives in Corsica, began feeding him a harsh tartar emetic, a poisonous antimony compound masked in lemonade. It was a standard medical purgative. The drink made Napoleon writhe on the floor in agony, but the dosings continued. A second physician, military doctor Archibald Arnott, suggested that the emperor might be helped by even more purging.

Today their judgment seems appalling; in fact, purging the stomach of a patient with stomach cancer seems downright malicious. And murderous. But in that day doctors routinely subjected weak, dying patients to copious purging, bleeding, blistering, and enemas.

When Napoleon's suffering intensified, Dr. Arnott mercifully administered ten grains of the toxic mercurial laxative calomel, more than three times the recommended maximum dose. Within hours, the former emperor was unconscious. He died at 5:49 p.m. that day, May 5."

Napoleon is laid to rest.

Publication of Napoleon's memoirs and those of his aides helped to lift a reputation that had fallen in the mud after the final abdication. Also aiding the resurrection of the emperor's reputation was the inability, in the years that followed, of either the allies or the restored Bourbons to markedly improve the lot of the average European. The remainder of the nineteenth century and the beginning of the twentieth would see many European revolutions, and eventually most of the old guard was swept away. Memories were perhaps more important than memoirs in restoring the luster to Napoleon's name. Veterans who had served under him looked back fondly on their days of glory. Memory tends to be rose-colored. Even such nightmares as the retreat from Moscow became glorious in the retelling. Few things in life give so much pleasure as the memory of suffering. The veterans' children and grandchildren listened to the wondrous tales and wished they could have been there.

Napoleon went to St. Helena as an outlaw and outcast—easily the most despised person alive. By the time his body was returned to France in 1840 to lie in a magnificent tomb, he had become his country's greatest hero.

A Mixed Legacy

Nearly 200 years after his death, historians have not reached a consensus on Napoleon. On the same library shelf, one may find scholarly books praising him as one of the greatest and most admirable men in history alongside equally learned volumes blasting him as one of the worst calamities ever to afflict the world. Most historians, of course, find some middle ground, balancing the man's virtues against his faults, his achievements against his failures, the good he accomplished against the evil he brought. Yet, even then, the very acts one historian praises may be censured by another.

Let us start with the one point nearly everyone can agree upon: as a military leader, Napoleon was unmatched in his own time. His string of victory after victory

Napoleon leads his troops to battle. History's judgment of his legacy is mixed, but all agree he was the greatest military strategist of his day. For Napoleon, Europe was the clay with which he tried to create his vision of history—with himself at the center.

proves the point beyond discussion. But how might he have fared in a different time or place? His lack of physical size would have limited him in a far earlier era, when hand-to-hand fighting with axe and sword was the norm, but his personal courage and boundless energy might have compensated. And, on many occasions, he demonstrated his ability to lead by example—a necessity among ancient warriors. Probably Napoleon would have made an excellent soldier in any time period preceding his own.

The nature of warfare has changed so much in the past two centuries that we may wonder how the architect of the Battle of Austerlitz might perform in our own time. The modern general is essentially an executive, managing huge ground, air, and naval forces, together with gargantuan supply lines. Though the general is ultimately responsible for all, the details of his plans must be executed by his subordinates. Napoleon was an able administrator within limits, but he showed a marked inability to delegate authority. And, he seems to have chosen his immediate subordinates on the battlefield more for their courage than for their intelligence or efficiency. Modern soldiers require all three. On the other hand, if thrust somehow into our own age, Napoleon might well have been able to change. A lifelong opportunist, he would have been flexible.

Unique to our own time is a tendency to judge men of war on the justness of their causes. We honor soldiers whom we deem to have fought on the side of the angels and ignore or even abuse those of equal valor and ability who contested for aims we find less noble. In recent American history, for example, the heroes of World War II (when the United States opposed a definable evil) are still held in high regard; equally brave and able men who fought in Vietnam (when, we have decided, the war itself was evil) are seldom remembered, much less honored.

Was Napoleon's cause just? Some historians have pointed out that the so-called Napoleonic Wars began long before Bonaparte achieved power, that France was attacked as often as it attacked others, and, that regardless of the opinions of other nations, the majority of the French people favored Napoleon's aggressive policies. On the other side are historians who maintain that Napoleon was in a position to bring peace to Europe throughout most of his reign yet insisted on conducting war. They note that he aimed to force all Europe under the fist of France and that he oversaw the systematic looting of conquered countries. These were hardly honorable goals, and, in his pursuit of them, several hundred thousand died.

His actions as emperor are a mixed bag. He is praised for his law code, for stabilizing government finances, for building roads and other public facilities, for his encouragement of business, and for his religious tolerance. He is criticized for his curtailment of individual liberty, for his censorship of the press, for his use of secret police, and for his Continental System, which brought ruin to many of his own people. Most of all, he is blamed for establishing a system of government that put all power into the hands of one man. His was the model for every totalitarian regime of the twentieth century, with inevitably disastrous results for the average citizen.

Napoleon can be admired for a vaulting ambition that saw no restrictions, while being cursed for not recognizing the limits

A bust of Napoleon in the likeness of a Roman emperor (left) and a portrait of him as a general (right). Like most important historical figures, Napoleon had within himself both good and evil, great gifts and tragic flaws. He was only a man after all, but a man who, to borrow a phrase from French author Emile Zola, "lived his life out loud."

imposed by simple morality. He can be called ruthless or simply opportunistic. His conquests made France rich but ultimately brought it low among nations. He was perhaps the most important single cause of the nationalistic movements that spread through Europe during the nineteenth century, but nationalism has proved to have both a good and an evil face. At any rate, it resulted as a by-product of his actions rather than as a goal he set out to accomplish.

In summary then, Napoleon possessed rare gifts of character and constitution. His ambition, opportunism, and courage allowed him to ride those gifts to unprecedented personal heights. That his legacy to humanity falls short of its possibilities may be charged to an excessive focus on his own career, at the expense of any great interest in his fellow humans. Had his vision been wider, he might be remembered not only as a great hero, but as a great man.

Notes

Introduction: The Great Adventure

1. *On St. Helena* [March 3, 1817]. Cited in John Bartlett, *Familiar Quotations*, Justin Kaplan, general editor. Boston: Little, Brown, 1992.

2. *Letter to General Lemarois* [July 9, 1813]. Cited in Bartlett, *Familiar Quotations*.

3. Marvin Perry, *Man's Unfinished Journey*. Boston: Houghton Mifflin, 1974.

Chapter 1: An Emperor and a King

4. Will Durant and Ariel Durant, *The Age of Napoleon*. New York: Simon & Schuster, 1975.

5. Editors of Time–Life Books, *The Pulse of Enterprise*. Alexandria, VA: Time–Life, 1990.

6. Jean-Louis Campan, *Memoirs of the Private Life of Marie Antoinette*. Boston, 1917. Cited in Durant and Durant, *The Age of Napoleon*.

7. Albert Mathiez, *The French Revolution*. New York: 1964. Cited in Durant and Durant, *The Age of Napoleon*.

8. J. Christopher Herold, *The Age of Napoleon*. New York: American Heritage, 1963.

Chapter 2: For Patriotism

9. Cited in Durant and Durant, *The Age of Napoleon*.

10. Napoleon, *Letters* (June 12, 1789). Cited in Durant and Durant, *The Age of Napoleon*.

11. F. M. Kircheisen, *Memoirs of Napoleon*. New York, 1929. Cited in Durant and Durant, *The Age of Napoleon*.

12. Durant and Durant, *The Age of Napoleon*.

13. Herold, *The Age of Napoleon*.

14. Durant and Durant, *The Age of Napoleon*.

15. Herold, *The Age of Napoleon*.

16. Durant and Durant, *The Age of Napoleon*.

Chapter 3: Fortune's Favorite

17. Herold, *The Age of Napoleon*.

18. Herold, *The Age of Napoleon*.

19. Durant and Durant, *The Age of Napoleon*.

20. Durant and Durant, *The Age of Napoleon*.

21. Herold, *The Age of Napoleon*.

22. Thomas Carlyle, *History of the French Revolution*, Vol. 3, New York, 1901. Cited in Durant and Durant, *The Age of Napoleon*.

Chapter 4: To Italy and Egypt

23. L. J. Gohier, *Memoirs*. 1824. Cited in Herold, *The Age of Napoleon*.

24. Durant and Durant, *The Age of Napoleon*.

25. Durant and Durant, *The Age of Napoleon*.

26. Herold, *The Age of Napoleon*.

27. Durant and Durant, *The Age of Napoleon*.

28. Jean Bourguignon, *Napoleon Bonaparte*. Paris: Editions Nationales, 1936.

Chapter 5: The First Consul

29. Francis Mossiker, *Napoleon and Josephine*. New York, 1964. Cited in Durant and Durant, *The Age of Napoleon*.

30. Louis-Antoine Fauvelet de Bourrienne, *Memoirs of Napoleon Bonaparte*. New

York, 1890. Cited in Durant and Durant, *The Age o f Napoleon.*

31. Durant and Durant, *The Age of Napoleon.*

32. Durant and Durant, *The Age of Napoleon.*

33. Herold, *The Age of Napoleon.*

34. Herold, *The Age of Napoleon.*

35. Herold, *The Age of Napoleon.*

36. Perry, *Man's Unfinished Journey.*

37. Herold, *The Age of Napoleon.*

38. Robert B. Holtman, *The Napoleonic Revolution.* Philadelphia: Lippincott, 1967.

Chapter 6: The Emperor Strikes

39. Time–Life Editors, *The Pulse of Enterprise.*

40. Time–Life Editors, *The Pulse of Enterprise.*

41. Louis Madelin, *The Consulate and the Empire,* New York, 1967. Cited in Durant and Durant, *The Age of Napoleon.*

Chapter 7: Decline

42. Louis Madelin, *The Consulate and the Empire.* Cited in Durant and Durant, *The Age of Napoleon.*

43. Time–Life, *The Pulse of Enterprise.*

44. Durant and Durant, *The Age of Napoleon.*

45. Michael T. Florinsky, *Russia: A History and an Interpretation.* New York, 1955. Cited in Durant and Durant, *The Age of Napoleon.*

46. Comte Emmanuel de las Cases, *Memoirs of the Emperor Napoleon.* New York, 1883. Cited in Durant and Durant, *The Age of Napoleon.*

47. Durant and Durant, *The Age of Napoleon.*

48. Jean Mistler, ed., *Napoleon et L'Empire.* Paris, 1968. Cited in Durant and Durant, *The Age of Napoleon.*

49. Alan Palmer, *Napoleon in Russia.* New York, 1967. Cited in Durant and Durant, *The Age of Napoleon.*

50. Perry, *Man's Unfinished Journey.*

Chapter 8: Fall

51. Durant and Durant, *The Age of Napoleon.*

52. Durant and Durant, *The Age of Napoleon.*

53. Durant and Durant, *The Age of Napoleon.*

54. Claude-Francois de Meneval, *Memoirs of Napoleon.* London, 1894–1895. Cited in Durant and Durant, *The Age of Napoleon.*

55. Louis-Adolphe Thiers, *History of the Consulate and the Empire of France Under Napoleon.* Philadelphia, 1893. Cited in Durant and Durant, *The Age of Napoleon.*

56. Mossiker, *Napoleon and Josephine.* Cited in Durant and Durant, *The Age of Napoleon.*

57. Mistler, ed., *Napoleon et L'Empire.* Cited in Durant and Durant, *The Age of Napoleon.*

58. Albert Sorel, *Europe and the French Revolution,* Garden City, NY: Doubleday, 1971.

For Further Reading

Compiled with the aid of Linda Tashbook, District Young Adult/Outreach Specialist, The Carnegie Library of Pittsburgh.

Julia Blackburn, *The Emperor's Last Island: A Journey to St. Helena.* New York: Pantheon Books, 1991. A fascinating description of Napoleon's life in banishment. Comparisons between the author's contemporary visits to the island and conditions during Napoleon's captivity depict the differences between modern and historical concepts of luxury and necessity.

Alan Blackwood, *Napoleon.* New York: Bookwright Press, 1987. Very simple, well-illustrated coverage of Napoleon's personal and public development.

Owen Connelly, ed., *Historical Dictionary of Napoleonic France, 1799–1815.* Westport, CT: Greenwood Press, 1985.

R. F. Delderfield, *Napoleon in Love.* New York: Simon & Schuster, 1979. A not-too-gossipy introduction to the women in Napoleon's life.

Albert Marrin, *Napoleon and the Napoleonic Wars.* New York: Viking, 1991. A dramatic, insightful look at Napoleon's development from childhood through ambitious young adulthood, emphasizing his opportunism.

Desmond Seward, *Napoleon and Hitler.* New York: Viking, 1989. Somewhat scholarly, but interesting for teens who have studied twentieth-century world history.

Jakob Walter, *The Diary of a Napoleonic Foot Soldier.* Garden City, NY: Doubleday, 1991. Excellent for teens, this easy-to-read narrative shows an adolescent coming of age as a self-assured draftee in the Grand Army of Napoleon, following him from the invasion of Russia through the horrors of the retreat.

Ben Weider, *The Murder of Napoleon.* New York: Congdon & Lattes; distributed by St. Martin's Press, 1982. Presents convincing evidence that Napoleon was subtly murdered by poisoning rather than conveniently dying of stomach cancer.

Works Consulted

Geoffrey Bruun, *Europe and the French Imperium 1799–1814*. New York: Harper & Row, 1938. Volume XII in the Rise of Modern Europe series, designed to give the general reader a reliable history of Europe from 1250. Emphasizes the Napoleonic system and Europe's reaction to it rather than an account of the personality of Napoleon or his battles.

Edward McNall Burns, *Western Civilizations: Their History and Their Culture*, Vol. II. New York: Norton, 1973. Excellent general history with a wealth of detail and illustrations.

Thomas Carlyle, *The French Revolution*, New York: Modern Library. First published in 1837, this near-contemporary account is still exciting reading.

David G. Chandler, *The Campaigns of Napoleon*. New York: Macmillan, 1966. For the student of military history. A careful, scholarly detailing of each of Napoleon's battles with attention to his thinking behind each decision.

Will Durant and Ariel Durant, *The Age of Napoleon*. New York: Simon & Schuster, 1975. The eleventh and final volume in the Durants' monumental *Story of Civilization*. Napoleon is the central figure, but the Durants find ample opportunity to explore the arts, science, politics, philosophy, manners, and morals of the period, all recounted in graceful prose with a fine eye for revealing detail.

The Editors of Time–Life Books, *The Pulse of Enterprise: Time Frame A.D. 1800–1850*. Alexandria, VA: Time–Life Books, 1990. This typical Time–Life effort combines a sprightly, accurate text with marvelous illustrations. The Time Frame series devotes a chapter each to historical happenings during the frame in several parts of the world. In this volume are "Bonaparte's Empire" and chapters on contemporary events in England, Latin America, China, and South Africa.

The Editors of Time–Life Books, *Winds of Revolution: Time Frame A.D. 1700–1800*. Alexandria, VA: Time–Life Books, 1990. This Time Frame volume includes solid chapters on the revolutions in both France and America.

Michael Glover, *The Peninsular War 1807–1814: A Concise Military History*. Hamden, CT: Archon Books, 1974. A complete account of the first "guerrilla war."

Norman Hampson, *The First European Revolution 1776–1815*. Norwich, England: Harcourt, Brace & World, 1969. One volume in another fine series, the History of European Civilization. Explores the roots of revolution through the European reaction to the rise of Napoleon.

J. Christopher Herold, *The Age of Napoleon*. New York: American Heritage Publishing, 1963. In twelve highly readable chapters, Herold explores Napoleon's personality and career.

Robert B. Holtman, *The Napoleonic Revolution*. Philadelphia: Lippincott, 1967. This account looks at the influence of the emperor on nearly all aspects of European life, showing that he represented the practical application of the ideas of eighteenth-century rationalism.

Charles Panati, *Panati's Extraordinary Endings of Practically Everything and Everybody*. New York: Harper & Row, 1989. Contains a harrowing account of Napoleon's last days.

Marvin Perry, *Man's Unfinished Journey*. Boston: Houghton Mifflin, 1974. Contains useful chapters on the French Revolution and Napoleon.

David Stacton, *The Bonapartes*. New York: Simon & Schuster, 1966. Napoleon is only one character in this interesting, 200-year biography of the entire family from its beginnings in Corsica down to modern-day survivors.

Arnold Toynbee, *A Study of History*. New York: Oxford University Press, 1972. A new edition, revised and abridged by the author and Jane Caplan. The author's insights are always valuable.

Robin W. Winks, *Western Civilization: A Brief History*. Alta Loma, CA: Collegiate Press, 1988. A short history of the Western world since the beginning.

Index

Age of Napoleon, The (Durant)
  advice to Napoleon from
    Paul Barras, 42
  love letter to Josephine, 48
  Napoleon as melancholy
    youth, 25
  Napoleon's oath of office,
    14
  Napoleon's promise to
    troops, 51
Age of Napoleon, The (Herold)
  Napoleon on human na-
    ture, 57
  Robespierre's goals, 40
Alexander I, Czar
  invasion of Russia and,
    83–85
American Revolution 16
Amiens, Treaty of, 68
Austerlitz, Battle of, 72–73
Austria
  defeat at Marengo of, 68
  defeat at Ulm of, 72
  defeat in Italy of, 47–49
  as gained by marriage to
    Marie Louise, 80
  as ruler of Italy, 44–45
  Treaty of Campo Formio
    and, 51

Barras, Paul, 40–41, 42, 52, 58
Bastille Day, 18
Bastille
  storming of, 17–18
Beauharnais, Alexandre de,
  12
Beauharnais, Eugene de (son
  of Josephine), 74, 90
Beauharnais, Josephine de
  (wife of Napoleon), 48,
  74
  at coronation of Napoleon,
    11–13
  courtship and marriage of,
    37, 39

death of, 93
divorce of, 79–80
domestic problems with, 57
Bernadotte, Jean-Baptiste
  Jules (crown prince of
  Sweden), 88–89
Blücher, General Gebhard
  von, 95–96
Bonaparte, Caroline (sister of
  Napoleon), 23, 73
Bonaparte, Elisa (sister of
  Napoleon), 23, 73
Bonaparte, Jerome (brother
  of Napoleon), 23, 73,
  74
Bonaparte, Joseph (brother
  of Napoleon), 13, 23, 25,
  57, 73
Bonaparte, Louis (brother of
  Napoleon), 23, 73, 74
Bonaparte, Lucien (brother
  of Napoleon), 23, 29–30,
  57, 59–60, 74
Bonaparte, Napoleon
  achievements of, 6–7,
    63–66, 100–102
  arrest as Robespierrist,
    35–36
  birth and family of, 22–23
  bravery of, 48
  as commander of Army of
    the Interior, 42–43
  Consulate and, 9–10, 58–60
  Corsican politics and, 26, 30
  criticism of, 91–92, 100–102
  death of, 96–98
  decline in generalship of,
    81–82
  defeat at Trafalgar of, 71
  defeat at Waterloo of,
    95–96
  defeat by allied forces,
    89–92
  defense of the Convention
    by, 40–41
  at the École Militaire, 24

effect on others of, 45, 47
Egyptian campaign of,
  52–55
as emperor, 9, 11–13, 69,
  79–80
exile in Elba of, 93
exile on St. Helena of, 96,
  98
as First Consul, 9–10,
  61–65
first war experience of, 33
French Revolution and, 60,
  63, 70
at height of power, 73–74
as hero to French, 52, 56,
  99
Josephine and, 11–13, 37,
  39, 48, 57, 74, 79–80,
  93
Marie Louise and, 79–80,
  93, 96
memoirs of, 98–99
politics of Directory and,
  42–43, 45, 48, 52, 56
popularity of, 63
promotion to general of,
  35
as propagandist, 82, 85
as road builder, 86
Russian campaign of,
  83–87
as schoolboy, 23
as second lieutenant, 24–25
siege of Toulon and, 34–35
signs of selfish ambition in,
  29
victory at Austerlitz of,
  72–73
victory in Italy of, 45, 47–51
Bonapartes, The (Stacton),
  The Bonaparte brothers,
  74
Borodino, Battle of, 85
Bourbons, 11, 12, 92
  restoration of, 93
Brunswick, duke of, 28

Buonaparte, Carlo Maria
(father of Napoleon),
22–23, 25
Buonaparte, Letizia Ramolino
(mother of Napoleon),
22–23

Campaigns of Napoleon, The
(Chandler), 50
Campo Formio, Treaty of, 51
Carteaux, General, 33–34
Charlemagne, 11
Commission of Legislation, 66
Committee of Public Safety
influence over army, 33–34
as supreme authority,
31–32
constitution
as drafted by Consulate,
60–62
as drafted by National
Assembly, 19
as drafted by National
Convention, 39
Continental System
blockade of England and,
74–75, 82–83
effect on France of, 75, 83
Corsica
as birthplace of Napoleon,
21–22
Napoleon's banishment
from, 30
Council of Five Hundred,
59–60

*Declaration of the Rights of
Man,* 19
Directory, 45, 48, 52, 56
fall of, 58–60
founding of, 42
Dresden, Battle of, 89

Egypt
campaign in, 52–55
scholarly achievements in,
53–54

Elba, 93
England
Continental System and,
74–75, 82–83
Egyptian campaign and,
52, 55
plan for invasion of, 52, 69,
71
reliance on exports by, 67,
74–75
rivalry between France and,
67–69
victory at Alexandria of, 55
victory at Trafalgar of, 71
Estates General, convening
of, 17
estates, three, people of
France and, 16
*Extraordinary Endings of
Practically Everything
and Everybody* (Panati), 97

First Estate, 16
France
as cultural center of
Europe, 14
economic decline of, 91
European opposition to, 30
extent of imperial, 73
Italian art taken to, 50–51
nationalism in, 77–78
as organized politically by
Napoleon, 61–65
rivalry between England
and, 67–69
sale of Corsica to, 22
three estates and, 16
without a sense of nation-
hood, 15–16
French army
inexperience of, 27
as inspired by Napoleon,
47–48
as isolated in Egypt, 55
poor condition in Italy of,
45
in Russian campaign, 84
French Republic, 9–10
French Revolution

achievements of, 66
after fall of Robespierre,
39–40
beginning of, 18
calendar changes and, 42
counterrevolution and,
30–31, 33, 40
effect of Napoleon on, 60,
63, 70
nationalism and, 77–79
radicals and conservatives
in, 26–28
Reign of Terror and, 10,
31–32, 36
Roman Catholic Church
and, 11, 19
under the Directory, 52
French Revolution, The
(Carlyle), fall of the
Bastille, 27

Girondins, 26, 32
government, under
Napoleon, 61–65
Goya, Francisco, 76
guillotine, 10, 28, 31–32

Italy
conquest of, 45, 47–51
as divided into many small
states, 44–45
French confiscation of art
from, 50–51

Jacobins, 94
Committee of Public Safety
and, 31
control of National Assembly by, 28
as middle-class, 39
rising influence of, 26
Jefferson, Thomas, 19

Kellerman, General, 12

legal system
    Napoleonic Code and,
        65–66
Legion of Honor, 69
Leipzig, Battle of, 89–90
*Little Known Facts About Well-
    Known People* (Carnegie),
    38
Louis XVI, King, 10
    acceptance of constitution
        by, 19
    arrest and execution of, 28
    attempts to restore power
        of, 27–28
    divine right of kings and, 14
    Estates General and, 16–17
    treason of, 20
    weakness of, 14–15, 16
Louis XVIII, King, 93–94
Louisiana Territory, 68–69

Marengo, Battle of, 68
Marie Antoinette (queen of
    France), 14–15, 32
Marie Louise (wife of
    Napoleon), 80, 93, 96
metric system, 69
Moreau, Jean-Victor, 89
Moscow, Napoleon's entry
    into, 85

Napoleonic Code, 7, 65–66, 93
Napoleonic Revolution, The
    (Holtman), 85, 86, 90
National Assembly
    Corsican self-government
        and, 26
    *Declaration of the Rights of
        Man* and, 19
    founding of, 17
National Convention, 39
    as defended by Napoleon,
        40–41
nationalism
    as fostered by Napoleon,
        77–79, 90

Nelson, Admiral Horatio
    victory at Alexandria of, 55
    victory at Trafalgar of, 71
Ney, General Michel, 94–96

Ottoman Empire, 53, 55

Paoli, Pasquale di, 26, 30
    Corsican independence
        movement and, 22
Papal States, 44, 48
Peninsular War, The (Glover),
    82
philosophes, the, influence of,
    19
Pitt, William, 73
Pius VI (Pope), 51
Pius VII (Pope),
    coronation of Napoleon
        and, 9, 11–13
Portugal
    guerrilla warfare in, 75–76
Prussia
    as ally of Austria, 27, 30
    defeat at Jena of, 73

Robespierre, Augustin, 35
Robespierre, Maximilien, 39
    as dictator of France, 32,
        35
    fall of, 36
    goals of, 40
Roman Catholic Church
    as First Estate, 16
    French Revolution and, 11,
        19
Rosetta Stone, 54
Russia
    Continental System and,
        74–75, 83
    defeat at Austerlitz of,
        72–73
    defeat at Friedland of, 73
    invasion of, 83–87

St. Helena, 96
Saliceti, Antoine Christophe,
    33, 35
Second Estate, 16
Sieyès, Emmanuel, 58–61
Spain
    guerrilla warfare in, 75–76,
        82
Study of History, A (Toynbee),
    46
Sweden
    alliance against Napoleon
        and, 88–89

Teil, General du, 33, 35
Third Estate
    Estates General and, 17–18
    as supporter of church and
        nobility, 16
Toulon, siege of, 33–35
Trafalgar, Battle of, 71
Turkey. *See* Ottoman
    Empire

Unfinished Journey (Perry),
    29

Villeneuve, Admiral Pierre
    de, 71

warfare
    changes in, 24, 76, 81–82
Wellington, duke of
    Portuguese campaign and,
        76, 82, 88
    victory at Waterloo of,
        95–96
Western Civilization (Burns),
    70
*Western Civilization: A Brief
    History* (Winks), 63
women's rights, 66
Wurmser, Count Dagobart
    Sigismund von, 48–49

Picture Credits

Cover photo by North Wind Picture Archives

Alinari-Scala/Art Resource, NY, 72, 79

Anne S.K. Brown Military Collection, Brown University Library, 41, 44, 77

Art Resource, NY, 12, 76, 84

The Bettmann Archive, 9, 10, 14, 22 (bottom), 23, 26, 28, 31, 32, 35, 36, 43, 52, 62 (bottom), 69, 91 (top), 92, 94 (both), 95, 97 (top), 98, 102 (left)

French Government Tourist Office, 97 (bottom)

Giraudon/Art Resource, NY, 13, 68, 80, 83 (top), 100

Historical Pictures/Stock Montage, 19, 24, 34, 40, 47, 49, 53, 55, 56, 60, 65, 83 (bottom), 87, 88

Lauros-Giraudon/Art Resource, NY, 46, 54, 64, 81

Library of Congress, 6, 58, 102 (right)

National Archives, 78

North Wind Picture Archives, 7, 8, 15, 17, 18, 22 (top), 25, 29, 33, 37, 38, 39, 50, 61, 62 (top), 70, 71, 73, 75, 91 (bottom), 93, 96

About the Author

Bob Carroll is the author of more than twenty books and over 200 articles primarily about sports history. His credits include *The Hidden Game of Football* (with John Thorn and Pete Palmer), *The Sports Video Guide, When the Grass Was Green, The Major League Way to Play Baseball,* and he was co-editor of *The Whole Baseball Catalogue.* In addition to writing, he is a sports artist whose illustrations appear regularly in several national publications. Mr. Carroll lives in North Huntingdon, Pennsylvania.